It can be one of the most frightening things a grown person may ever do. It can also be one of the most self-affirming. The honesty and trust it expresses have created chasms of alienation or steel bonds of love forged through complete acceptance. It is an issue that all Lesbian and gay parents must eventually face: coming out to their children.

Coming out to one's children is a relatively new issue. Although gay and Lesbian parenting is probably as common now as it was twenty-five years ago, the increasing visibility of gay families is a new phenomenon. Many more parents are now living openly homosexual lives. As Lesbians and gay men become an ever more widely recognized element in our society, we present a visible alternative to traditional heterosexuality — including alternative family structures. Therefore, coming out to one's children is a contemporary issue which has not previously been explored but whose timeliness is unmistakable. The coming-out of Lesbian and gay parents to their children redefines the structure of parent-child relationships in a unique way.

THERE'S SOMETHING I'VE BEEN MEANING TO TELL YOU

edited by
Loralee MacPike

The Naiad Press, Inc.
1989

Printed in the United States of America
First Edition

Cover design by Pat Tong and Bonnie Liss
    (Phoenix Graphics)
Typeset by Sandi Stancil

Library of Congress Cataloging-in-Publication Data

There's something I've been meaning to tell you : an anthology about lesbians and gay men coming out to their children / edited by Loralee MacPike.
        p.   cm.
    1. Gay parents—United States—Case studies. 2. Children of gay parents—United States—Family relationships—Case studies. 3. Lesbian mothers—United States—Case studies. I. MacPike, Loralee.
HQ76.3.U5T47   1989
306.874—dc20   89-8307
                                                                CIP

ISBN 0-941483-54-1 : $16.95
ISBN 0-941483-44-4 : $9.95

To my grandmother Josephine,
my mother Loretta,
and my daughter Gwynn:
The past and future of women's strength and love.

CONTENTS

PREFACE
by Gwynn Sawyer Ostrom
daughter of Loralee MacPike

I was sixteen when I found out that my mother Loralee MacPike, the editor of this book, was a Lesbian. We were spending a month in Europe; a college professor, she was giving a paper in Aix-en-Provence, France, and had invited me to join her. It was our first trip to Europe. She had gone early and spent some time in Holland with a "friend"; I met her (alone) in Paris, and we traveled, ending up in Aix.

Monday, August 28, 1978. Aix, France
Well, here I am in Aix-en-Provence, having a jolly time doing nothing (besides writing in this diary). Anyway, I'm very confused, mixed-up, and upset. Let me get right to the

point. I think that Mom's a Lesbian. Now, it's her life, and as long as she doesn't ask me to join her I really shouldn't worry about it. But I am. I don't know; I guess it's just against my principles (if I even can call them that). I'm not angry with Mom about it, but I don't think I can face her "partner" (if she even has one, if she even *is* one). I'm going to meet her next week and they've been roommates for a half a year and are going to be next year too. But that's not what is making me suspicious. I happened to read one of Barbara's postcards and it said, "I am lonely and cold without you." Now, I can understand the "lonely," but not the "cold." Unless they sleep together. Hmm. I don't know. Also Mom says she cares a lot for Barbara. I wonder in what way. Maybe my mind is just turning everything I hear into a negative sense. I hope Mom isn't a Les, but if she is she's not going to see much of me next year because I don't think I'll be able to stay in the same house as Barbara. Maybe I'm worried that all of Mom's love will now go to Barbara, but that's ridiculous. She loves me just the same even though she is having a relationship (no matter what sex).

The reason I can write this is that Mom is at a conference for teachers from all over the world. . . More later . . .

Tues., August 28, 1978. Aix, France
I think my suspicions have been confirmed; however, I'm not able to approach Mom yet about it. I don't think I ever can.

Barbara called last night. Yuk!

Thurs., August 21, 1978

I was right and when I get home I'm going to write Mom a letter.

August 31, 1978

Mom,

I am writing you this letter just to let you know what I think and feel and where I stand.

I have done a bit of "sleuthing," you could say, and have come to the conclusion (which I believe is correct) that you are gay. And I don't mean happy. It is very difficult for you, I'm sure, to understand what it is that I am trying to say.

I'd first like to make it clear that your decision in no way affects my love for you. I respect your decision and at the same time believe that it is really none of my business what you do, just as long as you do not try to induce me to join you, and I am sure that you respect my decision. It's not that I don't wish to get involved with your decision.

Every atom in me is wanting to say, "No. No. You're wrong," but I can't because I don't feel that what you are doing is wrong, for you. I really want you to know that I have no feelings of horror or pity for you; you've made your decision, and it would only prove detrimental to our relationship if I tried to make you see things my way. The only thing I want is for you to be satisfied and happy with your decision. The only thing I can say is that you shouldn't feel inadequate (if you even are) because of me, like you're not being a good mother or anything. Hogwash! Being a good mother and being a good lover are two entirely unrelated things and in no way do I feel that I am receiving less motherly care or less love because you have decided to be gay. (Do you mind me using that word, or would you rather I use "Lesbian" or "homosexual"?)

Anyway, I can assure you that your decision has not lessened my love for you, and that I don't believe that you are treating me unfairly.

I cannot honestly say that your decision has not bothered me at all, as it has, but I have assessed matters and have come to the conclusion in my mind that it doesn't matter that you are gay (or Lesbian, or homo). I love you just the same and nothing can change that.

Now that I have made a total mess trying to express my feelings, I shall wish you good luck. And please write back.

Love always,
Your daughter
Gwynn

P.S. By the way, if I am wrong, please forgive me because I have made a terrible mistake. Thanks! G.

Fri., September 1, 1978
I told her. And everything's okay now.

When I first suspected that my mother was a Lesbian, I was shocked — not at the reality of her being a Lesbian, but because I felt I was in competition with another woman for her affections. If it were a man, there would be no competition because I saw us (my mother and me and all women) as a separate and special group apart from men. Therefore, there would be no conflict of interest, so to speak, if it were a man my mother was in love with. Then why was I having such a hard time dealing with the fact that it was a woman she was in love with? I felt hurt because this was something I had found out for myself, and at the time it crossed my mind that if I had said nothing, she might never have told me herself — a lack of trust, perhaps? No. Looking back, it must have been that she was afraid to tell me, maybe for the very reason that I was shocked — because of competition.

I think that in the short period of time in France when, at sixteen, I suspected and had to deal with all of my confusing emotions, I grew up very fast. I suddenly realized that I was not the only focal point of my mother's life — there was someone else, someone on *my* level, a *woman*, to deal with. I began to see my life and those around me as somehow much more significant than before. I was no longer the "ordinary" teenager going through puberty. There was a lot more going on in my life — thoughts I never knew I would have. And when I confronted my mother with my suspicions and they were confirmed, I felt a great relief. I now knew the truth, so there was no doubt and no more confusion. I spent a lot of time thinking about what was going on before I approached her, as my diary entries show. It took me some time to convince myself logically that because my mother loved another woman, it wouldn't mean that she loved me less as a daughter. However, it's easier for the mind to say that than to make oneself believe it. I realized, though, that I would have to be an adult about this and not pull any childish games. I knew I could go through a routine of "spoiled and neglected daughter," but what would that accomplish? It would be even more difficult on my mother if I were to fuss and scream — besides having to swallow her emotions and answer my questions, she would have to deal with a blithering, irrational idiot-child. Instead, I vowed to keep my head and deal with the news intelligently and as maturely as possible. I really think that this helped out both my mother and myself.

My mother's coming out to me has had a profound effect on my life. At an early age, I learned quickly and with little pain to accept people as they are with no strings attached. I have become a lot more tolerant of people's actions and emotions because of my experience with my mother's coming out. I find it doesn't matter to me what a person says or does, but what s/he *is*. I believe that this is the key to cooperation and love.

I have also found that because my mother is a Lesbian, I tend to gravitate toward friends who I know will accept this as a part of my life and let it be. I used to base serious friendships on whether or not the person could handle the news that my mother was a Lesbian and be friends with her. I guess I thought at the time that it was a big deal to me that she was a Lesbian and therefore it might also be a big deal to others, so I always broke the news like I expected some big bomb to drop. It never did, though. Every single one of the friends I've told has accepted the news with aplomb and as if it was no big deal. I really think they all feel that way, too. No big deal. Not one ever expressed astonishment or disgust, or even indifference. All were understanding, and then we went on from there. I know now that that is no way to base a relationship, but it worked for me during my college years.

I no longer think about my mother as being "a Lesbian," although she lives with another woman and has bought a house with this woman. She is just my mother, and my friend. A wonderful woman. I think that her being a Lesbian has really opened up my world to a whole new way of thinking. It has expanded my consciousness to include many people I would never have met if not for my mother's associations with the Lesbian community. I have made friends with women who are delightful and sure of their sexuality as well as themselves as productive people — a rare sight today. So many people are so confused when it comes to sex and what they are themselves that it is refreshing to be in a room with such enlightened people as those my mother knows.

Her being a Lesbian has also taught me to be myself and accept myself for what I am. Growing up alone (which is how I view my childhood years — my mother and father both worked, and I essentially learned how to live by teaching myself and following others' examples) has allowed me a lot of time to be introspective and learn about myself and what makes *me* tick. Because I had little direction from authority, I was free to make my own choices and live my own life. And all the time I had a mother who was doing that too — first in her decision to get a Ph.D. and become a college teacher, then in her decision to become a Lesbian. I can only imagine that the independence I saw and learned helped me to deal with my discovery of my mother's Lesbianism; it has allowed me to accept whatever challenges have come into my life with relative ease.

Now that I am in my late twenties and married, my life is different from the lives of most of my friends. My husband and I have had a lesson or two in family get-togethers with new dimensions and potentially sticky situations that most newlyweds don't have to think about. But my ten years of having a Lesbian mother pretty well made it impossible for me to pick an insensitive or bigoted husband. And when our families gather, Mother and Mary are my parents as much as John's mother and father are his. We all visit back and forth, write letters, make phone calls, and share family stories. We're simply a family, joined by love, not convention, and we like each other as people, not as roles.

I have to admit I have felt apprehensive at times, knowing that I am married to a man. I originally worried, along with many people who don't understand much about Lesbians, that my mother chose women because she was rejecting men. We've talked about this — about her rejection of "male ways of being in the world," as she puts it, and about how in fact she doesn't like men who are sexist, racist, ageist, elitist, etc. — or women who are that way either. We've talked, too, about the nature of sexuality, which intersects with personal politics but is also independent of them. My initial worries that my mother might force me to be a Lesbian too seem silly now, but they were very real then, before I understood what I do now about human sexuality and about *my* sexuality. I think that when I learned to be comfortable with my mother's sexuality, I also learned to be comfortable with my own. And as time goes on, the difference in sexual orientation becomes less important. What is important is that mother and Mary have welcomed John with open arms (literally), and he treats them as if they were his own parents, with trust and love. I can't imagine a better family than that.

Since I forced my mother to come out to me ten years ago, we've developed a very loving, trusting relationship, one which has been strengthened by my knowledge of her Lesbianism and by the bonds of womanhood. My mother's openness about her sexuality has allowed us to be close friends in a way that very few people I know share with their mothers.

I think it is vital that a parent be honest with her child, and that honesty should extend to the declaration of sexuality. A child relies on a parent for guidance and yet also should view the parent as a friend. If values are an important part of a child's upbringing, the honesty that goes hand in hand with trust must be apparent to the child. Instead of hiding behind one's fears of openness, to gain trust and love and receive the same the parent should come out to the child and show his or her hand first. Honesty leads to honesty, trust to trust. Like parent, like child: do not expect the child to be honest if you can't be honest yourself.

Gwynn Sawyer Ostrom

INTRODUCTION

It can be one of the most frightening things a grown person may ever do. It can also be one of the most self-affirming. The honesty and trust it expresses have created chasms of alienation or steel bonds of love forged through complete acceptance. It is an issue that all Lesbian and gay parents must eventually face: coming out to their children.

Coming out to one's children is a relatively new issue. Although gay and Lesbian parenting is probably as common now as it was twenty-five years ago, the increasing visibility of gay families is a new phenomenon. Many more parents are now living openly homosexual lives. As Lesbians and gay men become an ever more widely recognized element in our society, we present a visible alternative to traditional heterosexuality — including alternative family structures. Therefore, coming out to one's children is a contemporary issue which has not previously been explored but whose timeliness is unmistakable. The coming-out of Lesbian and gay parents to their children redefines the structure of parent-child relationships in a unique way.

This volume attempts to explore that redefinition. It does so through the lives and words of the women and men who have taken the risk of making themselves known to their children. These are not third-person, second-hand recountings; they are not intellectual analyses or sociological explanations. They are the stories of what actually happened to people like me and like you when they told their children — often the human beings closest to them — that they were in this one important respect very different from most other parents. Some stories are long, complicated by a tangle of situations. For some people, the telling is an event with a beginning and an end, fitting well into what we as readers have come to expect from an anthology of life stories, while for others it is an ongoing process which eludes categories of narrative and forces us to acknowledge that life is not always a tidy story. I have consciously chosen a feminist methodology for gathering and editing these stories: I asked people to tell me what their experiences were, then looked for the patterns, philosophies, and politics that emerged. What I have tried to capture in this collection of coming-out stories are the voices of our gay and Lesbian communities, speaking to our children and in turn listening to them.

These voices are not monolithic. They are conservative and radical; they are rural and urban;

they are poor and comfortable and affluent; they are political and apolitical, religious and non-religious, prosaic and poetic, old and young, black and brown and white, angry and calm, assured and reticent. Only a few of the contributors are trained as writers, yet I think you will feel, as I did, the power of lived experience rising and animating the stories. This collection, more than anything, rings forth a truth of our Lesbian and gay lives which has not yet been spoken with the firmness, the vigor, the multiplicity, the infinite variety of these stories about gay men and Lesbians coming out to their children.

It is necessary to add a word about how these stories were gathered. Gay and lesbian publications all over the United States announced the anthology and asked for submissions. The writers included are all self-selected — they sent me their stories. Although I have been open to everyone's story, I have not sought manuscripts from specific "targeted" groups. So this volume does not even approximate a demographic cross-section of the Lesbian and gay community. You will notice immediately that there are many Lesbians and few gay men, many working-class women, no Asian-Americans. I have no explanation for the cross-section of people who wanted to tell their stories, although I can make a few guesses. Because more Lesbians than gay men live with their children, and because the mother-bond is traditionally believed to be stronger than the father-bond, it may be that more women than men are in a custodial and emotional position to come out to their children. Because it is currently fashionable in middle-class society to be "tolerant" of sexual orientation, it may be that coming out to one's children appears less significant to middle-class parents than to working-class parents, whose children often inhabit a less "liberal" world and who may therefore be more negatively affected by the knowledge. It is only within the past few decades that Black, Asian-American, and American Indian experiences (particularly women's) have appeared in mainstream American literature at all, much less Lesbian and gay Third-World experiences. Perhaps it is too early to expect an outflow of coming-out stories in these cultures.

Of course, these are only guesses on my part. But there are reasons why, in 1989 in America, a collection of stories about coming out to one's children contains contributions from some people and not from others. Until we have created in this country a society where everyone feels free to live out her or his inner self, where family is redefined as a group of people who bond together emotionally and share their lives, and where everyone's experience is seen as valid, interesting, and instructive, we will not have true multiplicity, in anthologies or in schools, lives, or minds.

So what I present to you here between these covers is not a "representative sample" but a series of truths which tell us where we are — today — as a culture within which one courageous group of people, long oppressed for being who they are, struggles to live the truth of their existence and to achieve the honesty and self-definition for which we all strive. In this way these stories truly represent gay and Lesbian parents who have taken what may be the biggest risk of all. If we show our children who we really are, will we lose them? This, of course, is a question Lesbian and gay children have long asked themselves about their parents. In this book, for the first time, we see the depth and breadth of the struggle of gay and Lesbian *parents* as they take that huge, often frightening, step and make the disclosure that can never be revoked.

Coming out to one's children is also a microcosm of Lesbian and gay existence in a heterosexist world. Most children of gays and Lesbians were born within heterosexual relationships,* and both children and parents grew up in a world that assumes the rightness of heterosexuality and often reinforces the invisibility of homosexuality in ways that make it particularly precarious for parents to disclose their sexual orientation. In coming out, we shatter heterosexist preconceptions. We make visible the inherent artificiality of the institution of marriage. We expose the unjustified privilege accorded to heterosexuals merely on the basis of their sexuality. We force a redefinition of the family, both through the roles we assume (or abandon) in our new family structures and through the evidence we so visibly present of alternatives to old family structures.

In these and myriad other ways, Lesbians and gay men stand at the forefront of the struggle against a heterosexist, patriarchal culture which has warped and limited human potential. We have made great strides toward creating for ourselves as individuals a respected place in a changed culture, one which embraces us as part of humanity's lovable, desirable multiplicity. We take the next step by telling the

---

*This will be less true in another decade, when children born to Lesbian co-parents may constitute a much larger percentage of children of gays and Lesbians.

stories in this anthology and by expanding our individual circles of honesty and love to include the next generation. They will inherit our good work and then shape a future on the basis of their own widened understanding and deepened capacity to love. In this sense, these stories are a landmark. Through them, and the brave and loving actions they represent, we are building the New World, for and with our children.

Loralee MacPike

I

FROM THE BEGINNING

When we think of coming out to our children, most of us envision an announcement, a disclosure, a change in our children's perceptions of us and the world. But this is not always so. As more Lesbians and gay men choose parenthood, coming out will more and more begin at conception and constitute a living process rather than a change in perceptions. The complex and often mystical communications between mother and unborn child can provide a matrix within which a parent's deepest self opens to the child. This communication can also occur with a co-parent who shares intimately and physically in the months of gestation.

As gay men and Lesbians enter more fully than ever before in history into parenting, more children will be born into a knowledge and acceptance of their parents' fullest, richest selves.

BABY UNBORN
Cathy

There are a lot of things I need to tell you, so
here is where I begin. Long before I ever decided to
have you, I met a wonderful woman named Brenda,
and we fell in love. This is not how the majority of
people raise their children; nowadays only a very
small number of special people bring children into the
world this way. Out of the love that Brenda and I
have for each other grew our desire to have you. You
may never know your father, but please remember *he
is a very special person*. I wanted a child, and he was
the person I chose, even though I was not in love
with him. When you were conceived, he had no idea

3

what my intentions were. I simply wanted a child whom I could share with Brenda. I never intended for your father to know that he was your father. But he was persistent and found out. Like Brenda, he loved you and wanted you; he offered to marry me, in order to keep you. But in the end, out of his love for you, he chose not to interfere. I'm very happy with his decision.

I suppose being pregnant and single is never easy, but being gay and pregnant is even worse. My co-workers ask a lot of questions; even our gay friends don't seem to understand and need to keep asking if we understand what we are doing. The few times Brenda and I have gone to the women's bar (no, I don't drink alcohol; I go for the socializing) everyone stared and whispered. People I don't even know ask questions!

Where do I give birth to you? I thought this would be an easy decision — choose a doctor and you're on your way. However, your birth seems to be in opposition to the medical profession's beliefs. As soon as they found out I was single and that the person I wanted with me during labor *and delivery* had no blood relationship to you, their answer was No! The doctors were willing to let Brenda be my labor coach, but they wouldn't let her hold my hand through the delivery. After tears and turmoil, I have decided to give birth to you at home with the help of a midwife. I feel lucky to have found a group of highly qualified midwives who make me feel very comfortable with my decision to have a home birth. Never once has one of them concerned herself with my lifestyle. I almost know they know, for they talk as if they understand and are comfortable with it.

The main concern of G.B. and Barb, the two midwives who will be with me during delivery, is that you be born healthy and into a loving family. We are certainly that!

I have just found out that my medical insurance would have paid for a hospital birth but won't pay one cent toward a home birth. I am having to struggle against the whole world in order to give you life.

MEGAN WAS BORN IN 1985, AT HOME. BRENDA DID HOLD MY HAND DURING THE DELIVERY, AND FOR TWO AND A HALF YEARS SHE HAS BEEN MEGAN'S OTHER MOTHER. FROM THE MOMENT OF HER CONCEPTION, I BEGAN COMING OUT TO MEGAN. SHE KNOWS I AM AS LESBIAN IN THE SAME TOTAL, INTEGRATED WAY SHE KNOWS I AM HER MOTHER. HER DISCOVERIES WILL NOT BE THE SUDDEN SHOCK OF A PARENT'S REVELATION, BUT THE ONGOING SMALL BRUISES OF THE PREJUDICE AND CRUELTY OF A WORLD WHICH WILL NOT ALWAYS ACCEPT ME AS MEGAN WILL. IT HAS ALREADY BEGUN. BUT ALREADY MEGAN IS STRENGTHENED BY HER KNOWLEDGE AND STRONG IN HER LOVE FOR THE WOMEN WHO MAKE UP HER FAMILY.

When Megan was a year old, Brenda and I split up. But Megan still refers to her as her "other mommy" and beams at the sight of her or of her photo. Brenda continues to spend every other weekend with Megan, and recently, as Megan has learned to use the telephone, they talk on the phone almost every day. And the three of us continue to do family things together. Megan's initial nuclear family is very much intact for her.

Only very recently has Megan become aware that she doesn't have a father. At my grandmother's funeral she yelled out, "Where's my daddy? I want my daddy." At first I was shocked and tried to explain that her daddy wasn't there right then. Later, at home, she said, "My daddy's name is Charlie." Charlie is a male friend who has been around since she was born, but he isn't her biological father. It seems Megan was thinking about the father *role* and not the person. Charlie is indeed a father-figure for Megan. I'm glad she recognizes her need for him and his filling of that need. Much of the time Megan refers to Brenda as her daddy. I'm trying to get her to call Brenda by her name, as "Daddy" isn't an acceptable title when we're in public.

Megan has heard the words "lesbian" and "gay" since she was born, but I don't emphasize them. I'm not sure how fully she understands what they mean; at two and a half, she certainly has no idea about their sexual implications. She does, however, know a lot about affection and emotion between women. Once when I was crying, she asked me, "Mommy, Liz hurts you?" Sometimes she seems jealous and tells my lovers, "Don't you kiss mommy." Or if we are sitting close, she comes to sit in the middle — just as she would with heterosexual parents. I do try to explain that I love women and care about them in a very special way, but that she need not feel threatened because they can never take her place.

Most important is what Megan has learned by being with me and my friends. She goes literally everywhere with me. She's been to a gay bar (a men's bar during daylight hours on a Sunday when things were relatively quiet). She has gone to a gay babysitter. She asks butch women, "Are you a boy?" I try to explain that they are girls too (I'm very straight-looking), but she doesn't seem to understand yet. Very seldom am I invited anywhere that Megan isn't also invited. She has heard a lot of gay-oriented conversations and sees gay people together quite frequently. She hasn't reached the age yet where these things can seem different or wrong. I'm sure all of this will surface eventually, but by then I hope she will have come to accept women loving women as such an integral part of her emotional life that she'll be strong enough to withstand the inevitable taunts of unkind classmates.

Megan my daughter, when you were conceived, you were conceived within the love of women. You are being raised within this same love. It is the best heritage I can give you. My choice to give birth to you has paid off with a wealth of happiness, joy, and love. Sometime when you are wondering why your father isn't around, don't feel sorry for yourself. Feel blessed — for you have two mommies.

INSIDE OUT
Shelly Rafferty

I

O little soul
i don't know you yet
but when you're old
i hope you know
that every day we loved you
almost to death
trying to keep you.

II

what will you be?
now a thought i long to caress
hiding in the warmth
of my lover
your mother

my life
        and hers
        mingling soon
        to bring you
        to light.

There is no delicate way to tell the truth about children conceived by rape — but that is how my daughter came to be. The circumstances are not important; no one can give my lover her innocence back. I could not heal her, nor make her rapist not be her rapist, nor help her forget that our sanctity had somehow been violated. Our being Lesbians does not make her experience different from that of other women. She knew shame, guilt, and, ultimately, anger.

But the presence of a child in her womb which we had not willed there was somehow different for us than for straight women; we had never expected to conceive — even by design — through intercourse. We were suddenly subjected to a violation of the integrity of our fidelity, and also to a sexual practice we had worked lifelong to avoid.

We had always prided ourselves on our privacy, our intimacy, the intentional secrecy in which we shared thoughts to which we alone were privy. We whispered wishes in the darkness of our bedroom, beneath the tangle of sheets, where we dreamed of a life where we had nothing to fear. One day, there would be a house for us, a piano for her, a study for me, and too, in the misty distance, still hazy and undefined, a nursery for our babies.

Rape changed all that.

Arran has other children. They were conceived and brought forth in another time, before me, before she knew she was a Lesbian. I knew those children too, and they knew me like a friendly aunt, because they were young and our situation was precarious, custody of these being an issue in Arran's relationship with her husband. For this reason, we did not live together, and have never lived together. It's been a hard life, but a necessary one.

It was September, the first or second day of the month, as I recall. Arran and I had been separated for almost 12 weeks, as we were attempting to relocate to a city farther south. She'd gone ahead to find a job, a house. I stayed behind to keep the cash flowing, continuing to work in a battered women's shelter, tending to the wounded and surviving.

One afternoon, Arran called me from the airport, asking me to come and pick her up. Her voice sounded strained, remote; her affect was flat and unenthusiastic. I hadn't been expecting her. Although puzzled, I ignored my instincts to focus on her apparent distress. I was so happy to hear her voice. I sped to the airport on my motorcycle.

Arran was notoriously careless about riding with

10

me, so I knew something was afoot when she put her arms around me and laid her head on my back, all the way to my apartment.

I was used to her quietness. Arran is very introverted, always casting about in the regions of the heart, the mind, the soul. All weekend long she didn't want to talk. She didn't want to do anything but make love. Her appetite was unabated. We stayed in bed from morning to night, and on again into the next sunrise. We said very little. She slept in my arms, close, like she hadn't before. She reached for me in her sleep; she pressed her body close into the protective circle of my arm. I told her I loved her.

She stayed quiet.

She went home Sunday night without telling me that she had been raped a few days before. It wouldn't have changed anything.

But the baby did.

Six weeks later, Arran called me from 600 miles away to tell me she was pregnant.

I grieved our losses; the telephone was heavy, unwieldy, as I sobbed into the mouthpiece anger, regret, helplessness and, ultimately, insight, deducing in a moment how it all had come to pass. A decision would have to be made. I needed to get South, to be with her. What would we do?

I had always had the pro-choice attitude that had come, bag and baggage, with my coming out among feminists, but Arran's experience was different. We hadn't ever talked about abortion; certainly, we never dreamed we would have to.

Within days, though, after searching my soul, I knew whatever choice I wanted Arran to make, her choice would be the one she had to live with. It

11

would have been wrong for me to choose. In the midst of this crisis, I needed to remind myself that Arran was the victim — not me — that she alone would bear the ultimate judgment of her peers, her family, her conscience and her God. I vowed support, no matter her decision.

I loved Arran. I had dreamed of sharing a baby with her. The father's identity was as immaterial then as it would have been years later, had we been given the opportunity to plan the pregnancy ourselves. When she told me she wanted to keep it, I knew we had been gifted. She trusted me; her incredible courage and faith were a testament to the strength of our relationship. We began to plan for our family.

I moved South.

I got an apartment near Arran's; at last, we began to sleep together frequently, and then we began, ever so slowly, to tell not only our baby about us, but also each other. We were going to be parents, together.

Together, we had chosen life for this fetus which, although not willed, was still wanted, would still bear a life to which we had given assent and affirmation. By some miraculous cosmic leap, we were able to transform the ultimate violation and robbery of self into something that was selfless, loving and ours.

More than anything, I needed Arran to confirm that the role that had been foisted upon me, but which I also willingly assumed, was a role that she wanted me to play. At first we struggled. I often felt insecure, wondering how we would help the baby identify me as parent, knowing that it would not live in my household. I can't remember how many times Arran told me not to worry, I was its parent, the baby would know. She calmed me, reassured me.

I knew that connecting with the baby was not something I could wait to do after it was born; the link to its existence needed to be established now, before it became a child with hair and eyes and skin and a nose that would never look like mine. What if it should not even resemble Arran? I remember praying for that, that at least we would be able to see Arran's face in the baby's — it seemed that fate owed us that minor concession. Lying beside her, I would place my hand on her stomach and talk to the baby. I told it stories, I sang, I prayed for its health, I caressed it and kissed it. I reached inside its mother and tried to touch it. I was amazed. Arran was beautiful then, perhaps more beautiful than in any time before.

I too was transformed. I bought cookbooks about making your own baby food. I bought bottles. I rubbed Arran's feet, went with her to the obstetrician, watched her diet. My library filled with baby books. I wrote lullabies and nursery rhymes and learned to sew. I drew butterflies and airplanes on cardboard, colored them, cut them out and turned them into mobiles. I studied name books, debating the significance of New Age, Biblical and ethnic curiosities. I prepared for a son: statistically that seemed likely. Arran's other children are all girls.

I brought wood scraps home from the lumberyard

to make blocks. I put safety hinges on all the drawers, bought everything in childproof containers.

In my bedroom, I started another project. I built a crib by hand. I made it a habit to keep a small ruler in my pocket so that when I was ever at K-Mart or Penney's or anywhere that cribs were to be found, I'd figure out a new piece of the puzzle. I measured mattresses and crib heights and slat widths. I copied the formula on paper and stuffed it in the pocket of my jeans.

As our fetus grew, I tried to think of ways the baby would know me, recognize me, not so much as just another familiar adult face orbiting around her, but as one of two who had had a voice in her very existence. For this baby I would not be just "Mommy's friend"; Arran and I had made a commitment that we often prayed would last a lifetime. But too, if that commitment should falter, I needed to know of ways that the baby would stay connected to me. This was going to be my baby as well as Arran's; I suddenly thought about stability, permanence, finding a better job, buying a house, and putting away money for the baby's college fund.

It was a while before I realized how necessary all of this preparation was — not because we soon would have an infant to share who cried and needed to be changed and fed, but because we as Lesbians had to create our own mechanism of conception and parenthood. These concepts needed to be firmly set in our minds in the event that, God forbid, someone tried to take our baby away from us with the assertion that we were not the baby's real parents.

As the time for Arran to deliver approached, my nights became more sleepless and worried. I desperately wanted to be with her in the delivery room, but in my heart I knew that that was not going to happen. I knew I had to trust her to find strength in the promises we had made through the past nine months. For us, it was only important that we knew that this baby was ours.

She stayed at home, exhausted, ate little, slept countless hours preparing for the labor that was ahead.

Suddenly, one day, she found herself full of energy. She drove to the nearby grocery store and spent $50.00 on Pine-Sol, Fantastick, Formula 400, Comet, Spic and Span, Murphy's Oil Soap, Pledge, Windex and a dozen new sponges. She spent the whole day scrubbing, mopping, disinfecting and dusting. She referred to this process as cleaning the nest.

It was a Sunday night, I think. As I dragged myself into bed around eleven, I prayed for sleep, a phenomenon that seemed foreign to me. I immediately fell into a deep sleep, the first I had experienced in weeks.

Around seven the next morning, I awoke to the phone ringing. It was Arran.

"Is it time to go?" My heart shook with sudden anxiety and alertness.

"No, darling. I'm at the hospital."

So I was not to be there.

"Is it over?" I asked.

I could feel her smile gently at the other end of the phone. "It's just beginning," she said softly. "It's a girl."

Rachel is almost four now; she knows me as "Shaba" (a kind of cross between Shelly and "mama"). She knows me like other children know their parents: I sleep with her mother, I take her to day care, I fix her meals. I taught her her first word "bus" and her second word "beer." Sometimes she gets mixed up and calls me "Mommy." I like that.

She has Arran's beautiful dark eyes and the same touch of rust in her brown hair. On days when she is especially mischievous, her double cowlicks remind us where her horns should be. I've watched her grow from a 7 lb.-7 oz. delight, through a chubby, rambunctious toddler, and into a delicate, slender pre-schooler. She's more gregarious than her mother (something we often remark that she gets from me) but has Arran's capacity for quiet, lengthy introspection. She has a long attention span. And perfect pitch. She sings and draws, and likes to ride her bike.

Coming out for us has not been a episodic thing, it has been process. We wanted to bear children together from the beginning. We wanted our children to be realized in the context of love, and this one was.

We have always been cautious around Rachel; but not, as some would imagine, to protect her from seeing us as Lesbians. On the contrary, we have worked very hard for her to see the connection

16

between us. She often sees us embracing, kissing. Her crib was in our bedroom; until she was almost 14 months, we made love without regard to her presence; we are gentle and quiet partners with one another. The phrase "I love you" is one she has heard from infancy, whether she was held in Arran's arms or mine. Arran has been especially good to me — although she is the biological parent, she has made every effort to let me be afforded the same intimacies she enjoys.

Lesbian parenthood is a concept to which we must make visible, tangible commitments, not to prove our point to straight people, but to be powerful, effective parents to our children. In our lifetime, and perhaps forever, models of straight parenthood will always overshadow models of child-rearing lesbians and gays. This fact alone — that straights statistically outnumber gays — can give unwarranted credence to children's concepts like "more = better" or "TV = reality." We must be intentional in the ways in which we reinforce basic parent-child interaction.

Young children internalize environmental messages in order to learn. If Arran and I are not intentional in our message, Rachel may conclude that she is the child of her mother and the man who fathered her other siblings. The other girls call him Daddy. Imitating her sisters, Rachel calls him that too, but I am confident that she recognizes me as her parent. Sometimes Rachel's sisters have expressed jealousy about me. They are less clear about my connection to Rachel. They are easily terrorized; we have chosen not to tell them about the rape.

We have never hesitated to take our baby anywhere with us. On count, she is probably equally exposed to straight people as she is to Gay people and environments. She is very verbal and inquisitive, and we encourage her to speak on her own behalf whenever possible. People often ask Arran (undoubtedly due to the striking resemblance between Rachel and herself) "Is she yours?" to which Arran uniformly replies, nodding in my direction, "Ours."

Despite her two separate households, Rachel finds her own dishes, toys, clothes, blankets, and bed without difficulty. These items do not migrate between households. Her reality of two separate parents living in different houses does not seem to confuse her. Arran and I provide an atmosphere of uncompromising consistency, expectations and rules no matter where she is. I am sure that it is the simplicity of this consistency which convinces Rachel more than anything that I am her parent.

For Rachel to have a greater consciousness about Lesbianism as she grows older, she will have her parents as models. Furthermore, the systems we use to nurture one another, to ensure a supportive network of women around us, and to inform our decisions about friends, toys, television and other media to which our child will be exposed all undergird Rachel's understanding of us.

It's important to understand that parenting is not a system of behaviors which evolves biologically, but is really the definition of the relationship between nurturing, caring adults and children. I often try to stress that the word "parent" is not only a noun, but also a verb. Parent is not something one just is, it is clearly something one does.

Not surprisingly, our Lesbian friends and acquaintances have often asked about our method of conception. Because it is a painful memory, we have chosen to respond simply that we are not willing to discuss conception. We try to stress that we decided to parent together and that the decision-making process requires introspection and gravity. Children should come by choice, never by chance.

When Rachel was just a few weeks old, Arran would bring her to me on the weekends. Arran went back to work. She'd let herself in before sunrise, my precious baby wrapped in her arms, and bring her into the bedroom. If there was time, she'd stay awhile, nursing Rachel, while I put my arms around her and rocked them both. Then after Arran left, Rachel and I would lie in bed together for hours, staring into each other's eyes, talking about her mother whom I love so much, ritual for rising: bonding.

II

THE ANNOUNCEMENT

I was lucky; my daughter announced my Lesbianism to me! Most Lesbian and gay parents aren't so lucky. Most have to find a way to tell their children — and most do it with an announcement: a talk around the dining table, a disclosure during a carefully orchestrated, pre-determined time, a snuggled moment before bedtime. The message of the announcement is always the same, but the ways of telling are as many and as varied as the men and women themselves. As you read these stories, you will see a variety of possible methods, styles, and settings for coming out. What is more striking, though, is the nature of the responses. Perhaps the worst fear Lesbian and gay parents have is that their children will reject them. But, as the stories in this section show, that isn't usually the case. Our children are more sophisticated, more knowledgeable, and more resilient than we are perhaps aware, as these tellings show.

THREE DEEP BREATHS
Miriam Carroll

Forty is not your usual coming-out age, but there I was, in 1970, ending a twenty-two-year marriage. I had been the typical mom of the 50s, trying to hold a hippie eighteen-year-old daughter, Lonnie, in line, sixteenaged Bruce away from the high school sugar cube crowd, our introverted eleven-year-old Cathy, on the verge of discovering boys, from saying "Eureka!" and myself from the decision whether or not to enjoy a quiet nervous breakdown. I chose instead to follow my new, healthy lesbian path. I was thoroughly scared but could no longer hold on to my old life.

Something, and to this day I do not know what,

23

precipitated the change. Suddenly I found myself fantasizing about my close women friends, and even obsessed over the beauteous Rosie for a couple of years before acting on my feelings, once Rosie moved far away and out of my life. I had plenty of time to make the right decision. I turned from the straight world to one that I had previously giggled derisively at: the gay scene.

Rebirthing, like the words "hyperactive child," had not yet become a fad. I was the model for both concepts. When I completed creating the egg, I scrambled forth as a baby dyke, ready to explore more of my awakened interest and sexual attraction for women.

Fate was kind. I started attending Daughters of Bilitis meetings in Boston, to learn what gay life was all about. Who were these women? How did they relate to each other? Could I find a place for myself? Would anyone want to live and love with me? I was most curious to find out how women made love, of course. My only experience was monogamy, and the thought of single life never entered my head. I made it known that I was available and sat back to see what would happen. I'm basically aggressive, so when Ginger's path crossed mine, and she appeared receptive, it wasn't long before answers started coming, along with my body.

My first new home was to be in Lowell, Massachusetts, 28 miles from the school where I had been a teacher for many years, in New Hampshire. I drove my first commute one frosty December day, with the sun brightly sparkling the newly fallen snow. I felt beautiful, and full of myself.

George, my husband, had been quite interested in

my gradual progress away from him. We considered our views quite modern, and as the years passed, we had even taken separate vacations. But we were not liberated enough for the wife-swapping going on in the 'burbs we lived in. I'd have been curious about the wives, but not able to handle the consequences.

As my feelings intensified, George and I discussed the minutest details. First, I thought I was bisexual, which he would "allow." At this point, it would have been nice to have a little woman in the attic to play with, so I could have kept my marriage intact.

Full-blown Lesbianism meant divorce. So be it. I was only kidding myself about being bisexual. I wanted that little woman in his space on the bed.

On a trip to a singles resort the summer before I moved out, Lady Luck sat me at the pool next to a sighing, lonely woman from New Jersey. I politely asked if she'd like a fine man to wed. She was definitely interested. I learned she fit many of George's needs: she was well-educated, had three children about the same age as ours, two girls and a boy, played bridge (his obsession), was financially secure, and was Jewish. The fact that she had a large chest was my going-away gift to George, the icing on the cake, as it were, after years of leanness. I told her I was leaving for a woman's love and needed someone to do George's laundry. I did not mention the ten-room sagging farmhouse, eight acres of lawn, numerous dogs, or the confused small child who would remain at home.

Love took its course, and 11 PM long distance phone calls (when the rates were lower) started cluttering up the bill. I scurried to my lawyer and packed my things. George's attention to my needs waned as his new love affair burgeoned. That was OK with me. He felt way before I did that I was interested in women. He thought that was the reason I was not jealous of his little office affairs. In truth, I did not know of them. I simply am not a jealous person.

We enjoyed an amicable divorce, deciding that the farm, when sold, would be my money. I'd have custody of Cathy, though she would remain home to continue school without disruption, and there would be a new small car in my future. I needed no alimony, as I'd continue teaching. I moved out, #2 moved in, and they were married the day our divorce became final in March. He never caused me any problem thereafter. The children, however, think he's changed, as he has become quite parochial in his outlook.

The kids met and accepted Ginger as my new friend. Bruce had a year to go until graduation and was old enough to weather our breakup, although the real reason was withheld. We told them it was a worn out and tired relationship which needed to be ended, even if the deep affection remained. Lonnie, the oldest, was already abrasively independent.

There was one very hard day to live through, when George and I told Cathy of our impending split. She had known a stable, loving environment free of shouting matches or craziness on the part of her parents. She felt secure thinking it was forever to be thus, even though few of her friends enjoyed original parents. Now she felt reduced to the common denominator of their broken homes.

Whenever I go back to visit the farmhouse, I can still feel the pain of Cathy, writhing in agony on the floor. My sorrow for that long-ago eleven-year-old remained in my heart, but there was nothing we could do to alleviate that pain. We tried our best to let her know she would be loved and that none of it was her fault.

It soon became apparent that Cathy was having problems. She started skipping school and hitting the funny cigarettes. The new wife could not handle her, so the old wife and her new lover took her in. Now we were faced with reality; how to break "the news." We decided to call in a lesbian therapist to explain things in the proper psychological language. Cathy's comment at the end of the "There are many ways to love" speech was, "It's OK for them but it sure isn't right for me!" We felt that was fair enough.

Ginger thought she could relate to Cathy because she, too, came from a broken home. She tried every which way to interest Cathy in various activities. We brought her dog to live with our growing menagerie. Nothing came of these ministrations but a frosty aloofness and internalized behavior, isolating herself even further.

Those were the days of "rapping," but whenever I attempted to knock, there was no answer, only a turned gaze and silent mouth. Cathy would not, could not, express herself. She confided in no one, not even her brother and sister. She was travelling with me to her old school, which kept her from making new friends.

As time went by, Ginger and I went back to New Hampshire, to live in a mobile home on a mountainside, where we established a kennel and cattery. There would have been plenty for Cathy to do, but nothing interested her except her first boyfriend, found at the local school she now attended. It was a small town where everyone knew everyone's business, a small town where the fact of two women having only women visitors was duly noted. Cathy and her friends spied on our group meetings. I think it was easier for her to be on "their side" when the innuendos came down on her. I know she was protecting herself, but we have never fully talked about those days.

She ran away, went back to George, then returned to our tiny community to live with a minister for awhile.

We stumbled along for five years. George divorced again, then married his secretary, a motherly woman who had no children. Finally Cathy had an adult on whom she could lean. I felt glad she was opening up to a sympathetic ear. I knew if Ginger and I kept our love for her visible in spite of all she could throw at us, someday she would be able to return it. It took another five years. To Ginger, I offer high praise for her effort.

Cathy grew up, married and had a baby before the flow of mother-daughter love was totally reestablished. Today, she has problems, but the past is not one of them. Once she had her own identity established as wife and mother, she had no further trouble with mine. She is the only one still in contact with Ginger. Loving persistence paid off.

Bruce came to visit us about six months into my new life. He brought along his current girlfriend, a student nurse. As they were about to depart, he turned and asked, "By the way, are you two lovers?" Speech left me. I had not been ready for a way to present this to the other children. Ginger calmly said,

"Yes." Bruce responded too quickly, "That's what I thought." Again he moved to leave, but had a smirk on his face I did not like. Ginger shot me a "Do something!" look. I quickly regained my self-confidence and boldly spoke.

"Not so fast, honey. Let's sit down again and get it out in the open." I did not mind that the young woman listened in silence. It would be an enlightenment for her.

With Ginger's interjections from time to time, I explained that a change had come over me, that something reversed itself completely in my personality and sexuality. Whereas I thought my sex life dead with his father, I joyously discovered new responses to lovemaking with Ginger. I was complete, happy and growing in new ways. Although I was sorry to cause pain to my family by ending a comfortable marriage, I hoped he would realize I needed to have the freedom to choose the course of my life.

The conversation went well. Bruce was a well-adjusted young man and seemed to understand. He needed time to digest this information. I was always pleased that my children never perceived me as a stereotypical, conforming mother, but maybe this was going too far. His stepmother told me he spent three days holed up in his room, but I never confirmed this.

Bruce seemed to feel an undercurrent of polarization between George and me, in spite of the fact that he knew we enjoyed an excellent relationship, as before. Our emotional bond took much longer to break than the physical one. He never cared to hear me talk of the new directions I thought George was moving toward. Nor did he wish to hear

George say anything about my life. To remove himself from this dichotomy, or possibly from being judgmental of either parent he loved, he left New England in his sophomore year of college for Ohio and the start of his own fulfilling adult life. He may have detached his body, but never his love. Today he is a superb dad and husband. A subtle sense of humor sparkles from his dark, intelligent eyes.

The oldest was the last to know. After opening to Bruce, I knew it was imperative to reach her, too. At this point, Lonnie was a rebellious eighteen-year-old, who had left home for her own apartment the previous year. She did not like the few house rules we had, such as washing dishes or keeping a somewhat tidy room. She graduated from high school, supporting herself by working in a sandwich shop, and had a donation box on her table.

I did not care at all for her unsavory friends. Her boyfriend was an alcoholic, dragging her down. She said she wanted a bottom-of-the-barrel type so that she could uplift his spirit, but of course this was not true. Somewhere along the line, she lost her sense of self-worthiness.

One awful night, when I was sleeping at the farm with Ginger, George having gone to New Jersey, Lonnie burst into the bedroom crying hysterically. Larry had been killed in a car wreck, driving drunk and severely injuring the other occupants. I consoled my daughter in my arms, silently thanking The Power they had had a fight and Lonnie was not in the car.

She seemed to grow up after that. Her next choice was a slender, quiet introverted young man. I liked

Danny, for he and I shared a common birthday. An Aquarian I could understand. Lonnie became engaged. Now it was a good time to talk with her about me. I repeated almost verbatim in the manner I had spoken to Bruce. She, so fiercely stabbing for her own independence, accepted mine with no problem.

Exhale.

After all, I recalled her saying as a child that I was not the plastic mommy so many of her friends had. Her response now was, "I'm so pissed you told me last!" How I hated THAT word, new to American slanguage. But, as her way of life as a full-blooming flower child attested, any lifestyle was OK as long as you were alive.

A day or so later, her fiancé put his arm around my shoulder and said, "Why did you wait so long to tell us? I loved you before you told Lonnie, you know. Nothing could change that." I was pleased but surprised. I had wanted to be oh-so-delicate with this Catholic fiancé of my Jewish kid. Not to worry, bless 'im.

Lonnie hastened into marriage and two delicious children. She was too overpowering for Danny, whom she divorced. He remarried a woman more to his calm ways, while Lonnie chose a man who loves her very much and can contain her volatile nature.

How lucky can a lesbian mother be? Maybe it's because the foundation for loving trust was created in those difficult, elusive growing years. Maybe it was the determination to always be available to listen to them. Maybe Ginger helped, in spite of her sometimes negative outlook. Whatever. By my children, I am blessed with love and acceptance of my lesbianism, independence, and sometimes outrageous behavior, and return it in full measure.

Today, six hundred miles separate us from hugs and kisses until we meet a few times a year. But when we do get together, you can bet on this: love blooms like a thousand-petaled chrysanthemum.

What about my parents? grandchildren? you ask. Well, that's another story . . .

COMING OUT TO MY KIDS
Martha Ficklen

I've always been out to my kids, I have told people; but what I remember about telling isn't always the same as what they remember hearing.

I have two sons, both grown now — 27 and 24. The time that all three of us remember my coming out to them was at the kitchen table the day after I came home from a week in New York City with the woman who is now my mate. Their father was also at the table, and the four of us planned our separation. At that time I thought it meant only a separation of my husband and me, but in another year I left town and the other three stayed in that home. I came to St. Louis to live with my lover.

In the summer of 1974 I attended a workshop for women writers in upstate New York. For two weeks I experienced the exhilaration of talking with other women about writing and living and ideas. This set a very supportive scene for me to meet the woman that I had been corresponding with for about seven months. We had first exchanged letters, then tapes and photographs and telephone calls. By the time we agreed to meet in New York I felt in love with her. When we met, I soon knew she was the person I wanted to live with. Before returning home, I stopped to visit friends in rural Pennsylvania. Joan and Jean had lived together for over ten years, and they introduced me to other couples who had been together for lengths of time varying from four years to twenty-two years. All of these experiences that summer led me to the courage to ask for what I wanted: freedom from my heterosexual marriage.

My husband had already known about my feelings for other women. My sons had been with me in Spain one summer when I spent two months in the home of a lover. The boys slept in one bed, she and I in the other, in the same room. We were openly affectionate in words and actions, but the boys were only nine and six years old. After that summer, I returned home with them, and other relations I had with women were more private. I felt that I was "out" to them, but there was seldom any comment about it. The older boy recognized that I loved women, and he occasionally spoke lightly of "one of Mom's crazy girlfriends." The younger boy sensed my impatience with his father. We all felt the tensions of my

34

growing frustration in our family life, but we also felt a loyalty to staying together. My husband and I came from families where divorce didn't happen. I didn't want the responsibility of breaking up our family. Finally I realized that I would have to do it.

At the kitchen table discussion we all cried. Only the younger boy was angry, or acted angry immediately. When I told him I hoped he wouldn't get into fights if anyone said something to him like, "Your mother is a Queer," because I am a Queer, he promised to shut up anybody who dared to say it.

My husband moved into an apartment that summer, and the boys and I stayed in our house. In St. Louis, my lover and her husband were also planning their separation and the sharing of their two children. I visited her in August and met her kids. They knew we had a loving relationship and began calling me "mother's best friend." When we shut the bedroom door, her daughter Jenny called in to us, "I know what you're doing in there."

My sons and I visited St. Louis that Christmas. I had started looking for a job in St. Louis. We stayed in the house with my lover and her kids, and everyone got along fine.

By the summer I had a job in St. Louis lined up, but my sons had decided they wouldn't move with me. They liked St. Louis, loved Nan and her kids, but they didn't want to leave their friends 1000 miles away. I suspected they also figured their father needed them more than I did. I regretted their decision but realized that I would go ahead with my plans to move.

My lover and I found an apartment together. Her kids would spend two to three days with us each week and the rest of the week with their father, who was still in town. My sons visited before their school began in the fall, then returned home to their father. All my spare dollars went to paying airfare for them to visit during Christmas vacations.

In April we moved into our house, where we still live. My boys came to spend the summer that year and for the next several years. My youngest son, Andrew, lived with us one school year, but he preferred his hometown and old friends. Honoring each other's choices hasn't always been easy for Andrew and me, especially when it meant separation, but neither of us questioned the other's right to choose.

Andrew, Jenny and Bobby came to us one summer and asked us to take off the shelves books with obvious titles, such as *Lesbian Nation* and *The Joy of Lesbian Sex*. They didn't want to have to answer the questions of anyone who came in to visit them, though most of their friends knew about us and were comfortable with knowing. We did put the books away, so for a few years some of our books were in the closet although we were not.

We have three favorite stories of dyke privilege in our family. My older son, Teddy, came to live with us to attend college. In his first semester he enrolled in a class, Intro to Women's Studies, where he met the woman he married five years later. He didn't need to buy the books for that class. They were already on our shelves.

My lover's son Bobby applied for a job at a restaurant owned by two dykes. When they interviewed him, he told them, "My Mom's a Lesbian." He got the job.

My younger son picked up a girl in a bar in Virginia Beach one summer who was grieving over her mother having come out to her. "My Mom is a Lesbian, too," he told her, and took her home to look through his photograph album at our pictures, our happy family.

OUR TRIP TO CHICAGO
Stephen Brammeier

My eight-year-old son has just spent the better part of yesterday vomiting. I had given him a bowl but he managed three times on the rug and once on his bed. He had diarrhea on the rug and wet his bed. We are leaving for a two-week driving vacation in four days. I am meeting a computer salesperson at my office tomorrow to make a final decision about spending $20,000 to bring my office operations into the computer age. The autoclave (sterilizer) also may have taken its last breath of the decade. My twelve-year-old begins his first baby-sitting class at Children's Hospital in the morning and he is feeling neglected because of all the time and attention given his vomiting brother. I'm trying to decide whom I should spend the little time and emotional energy I have this weekend with — my twelve-year-old son or my lover.

Becoming a parent and being Gay involved denial and a desire to change. Part of that process included sharing my fears with my future wife. My "problem" became one we would share and solve together. Looking back, I also believe that within our relationship, my Gayness became a safety factor that my wife also knew would bring me back to her and thought would never threaten her.

We were married for four years before the birth of our first son, Benjamin. These first years involved discussions about me, my fears and gyrations trying to understand myself. We were happy at times. I had fantasies to torment me and a rare contact that I would tell my wife about. The conception of our first child came during increasing fears and questions about myself.

The joy and excitement of experiencing the pregnancy and assisting in the delivery of my first child is unequaled by other joys. His presence decreased fears for a while; there was not much time to worry.

At seventeen months Ben was diagnosed as having Chronic Granulomatous Disease of Childhood (CGD). This is an inherited blood disorder. The method of inheritance is mostly X-linked recessive. At the time of his diagnosis in 1977, 30% of the children were not expected to live past three years and most would not live past young adulthood. Generally a child would succumb to a chronic infection from bacteria or fungus (viruses pose no increased threat). For a while we were lucky; Ben was healthy his first fifteen months.

The next two years involved a major adjustment as we adapted to the constant possibility of serious illness and maybe the death of our child. The support and caring of a congregation from a small Lutheran church was instrumental, but the religious contact also seeded questions about patriarchal Christian religion, in particular as it related to my child's illness, suffering, and possible death.

And then there was the question of whether we should have more children. Discussions with physicians informed us that should we wish more children, we had 25% chance of a boy with CGD, 25% chance of a girl who would be a carrier but not physically affected. The medical profession's answer was for my wife to become pregnant and abort any male fetus. However, they could not tell us if the fetus would be affected with the disease. We did not consider these reasonable alternatives.

My second son Joey's conception was not actively sought, but not specifically avoided. My wife's cycles were very infrequent and so was our intercourse. The pregnancy was emotionally difficult, and the birth traumatic for we were faced with another male child with CGD. Immediately after his birth in 1980 he was taken into isolation for 24–36 hours before his status and health were determined. He was literally tortured with numerous blood draws, etc.

From birth, Joey has had more problems than

Ben. At one year, he had surgery to open his chest and remove potentially infectious fluid from around his heart. The main trauma occurred in 1982 when from May until October, between the two of them, they were in the hospital eighty-four days. There was one weekend when both of them were hospitalized, and no longer than two weeks with both of them at home. Ben (six) had a case of pneumonia. Joey (two) had a variety of lesser problems but ended the summer returning from a short-lived vacation in Florida not being able to pass food through his stomach. It was painfully clear that our lives were governed by the day-to-day health of our children. We were often asked, "How do you do it?" (keep up with the demand of chronically ill children). My answer was, "I have no choice." But I worried . . . How long was I going to be able to keep up and would our marriage sustain the stress of two chronically ill children and a husband struggling with his sexuality?

During the years the boys were growing, I was beginning my own veterinary practice. In 1978 we moved into the neighborhood near my practice. This formerly failing neighborhood is like a small town within the city. We became a very visible family. I rehabbed a vacant service station for my practice and became active in grass-roots politics. My wife taught in a local school. The boys' health problems became common topics of discussion with my clients, neighbors, and friends, many one in the same.

By the fall of 1983 I realized that I could not much longer sustain myself in the closet. I needed the amount of energy it took to cope with hiding and suppressing my Gayness for more positive parts of my life. When my children were ill, the emotional and

41

physical demands were enormous. My Gayness and the difference in the way we handled the stress of a child's illness kept my wife and me from sustaining each other through those times. Ben and Joey needed and deserved the most I could give them. Holding back the Gay part of myself not only took too much energy, it also denied them knowing me. If they should die soon I wanted to be the best I could for them — and for me.

With the help and support of a group of people attending a class on Changing Masculinity sponsored by the St. Louis Organization for Changing Men, I gained the strength to accept being Gay. Through an exposure to and initial understanding of feminist writings and ideas, I began to identify some of the feelings women wrote about as the things I had felt as a child. Accepting my Gayness and verifying myself involved a broader understanding of prejudice and suppression in our society.

The ending of my marriage was caused in part by my being Gay, but it was also caused by my changing perspectives and values. I wanted to be more involved in my children's lives. Quality time is not predictable, and a quantity of time is needed to appreciate the quality. Children change subtly, and I needed more time to appreciate those changes. If they died next week, I wanted to give them baths, fight with them, tickle them, talk to them, hold them, touch them and love them.

Although I was honest with my wife from the beginning, when the divorce came it was predictably not easy. In retrospect I say predictably. At the time I thought we could divide our possessions and share parenthood of Ben and Joey. It was a little over two years before we were finally divorced.

From the time I moved from the house, the boys spent Tuesday and Thursday nights and every other weekend with me. After the long divorce process, we had joint custody and the boys spend half time with both of us. It is difficult, at times, maintaining the level of communication with my ex-wife necessary for the joint custody to work, but it is worth it.

Divorcing in the social and business environment we lived in was very visible. Also, I had chosen not to hide any longer. I only flame in selected environs, but I smolder a lot; my Gayness was quickly becoming common knowledge. I feared that Ben, now eight, and Joey, four, were going to be "informed" sooner or later, and I wanted the information about being Gay to come from me.

My memory of the boys' health situation in 1985 is not clear. Obviously, there were no major problems. I believe Joey was having prolonged episodes of leg pain that were difficult to diagnose but eventually stopped. On Labor Day weekend in 1985, fifteen months after my wife and I separated, I took Ben and Joey to Chicago.

There were many ideas I wanted to share. I wanted them to understand discrimination and sexism; I wanted to be able to give my thoughts and guidance to compete with what they are bombarded with every day. It was also important to me to help them understand that I knew I was Gay and that they too would know about their sexuality later. I wanted to let them know that most likely they wouldn't be Gay. Most of all I hoped we could build relationships that would allow us to talk about my and their sexuality. Ben was getting ready to begin fourth grade, and I knew that developing sexuality issues, boy-girl interactions and peer pressure would soon become important parts of his life. I was also feeling a need to begin to incorporate my social life, i.e., who I was dating, with my life as a father. I had decided that now was the time to tell the boys that I was Gay.

We sat in a generic Holiday Inn hotel room just off Michigan Avenue in downtown Chicago. The discussion began like most others by my announcing that I wanted the T.V. off. Thus primed for an "important" talk, the boys sat next to me on the bed, and I began my coming out talk.

I was scared. I had a nine-year-old serious person and a five-year-old "wild man" to talk to simultaneously. I talked about the end of the marriage. I talked about being grown-up and having another grown-up to love. We talked about their mother dating and I explained that when I found someone to love it would be a man. I wanted them to know because I loved them and it was important that they be able to meet the people I was dating. I don't remember specific who-said-whats, but I do remember hugs and "I love yous." I felt accepted, and "Could we please turn the T.V. back on?" Three years later they still remember our trip to Chicago and the food being cooked on the table at the "Chinese" restaurant and how Ben threw up afterwards and their dad told them he was Gay.

It turns out I was right in my belief that one way to nurture my children is to share myself with them. Remembering the experiences of my own childhood

44

and being willing to talk with my children has furthered heart-to-heart discussions. Sharing my own feelings and fears with my children has been risky, but my confidence has always been returned.

One night when Ben was seven, he was taking a bath. The tub was almost big enough for him to swim. I sat next to the tub on a bench. The house was old and the bathroom large. The stained glass french doors opening onto a second floor porch encouraged lingering baths and pleasant self care. I sat watching Ben slosh back and forth in the tub remembering childhood experiences that I wanted to share, and wanting to inquire about his life.

I told him about a girl who lived across the street from me when I was about five. We used to play on her swing and also in her garage. Mostly we would play that Mighty Mouse was in her garage. But one time I remember taking down our pants and seeing where each other went to the bathroom. We even touched each other's genitals. I touched her vagina and she touched my penis. I was frightened and thought I had done something wrong. I didn't tell my parents because I knew I would get in trouble. I felt bad. I was telling him this because if anything like that happened to him, I didn't want him to feel bad. If he wanted to talk to me he could and I wouldn't be angry. If he had questions about his penis or my penis or what a girl's or woman's vagina was like, we could talk about those things.

He said, "O.K." and when I asked if anything like that had happened to him he said, "Yeah, but her bathroom is too dirty." He spoke of an incident two years earlier with the girl across the street. Ben alluded that he declined participation, saying "I'm not

45

that kind of boy!" I cherish the memory of this discussion.

My openness with the boys has led to their growing awareness of the realities of life. Just this year, Joey (now eight) asked me why one of the current presidential primary candidates is talking about putting Gay people into concentration camps. I am concerned that this is a large worry for an eight-year-old, but how much better that he talked with me. A bond exists between us that would not be there if I hadn't shared with them.

Ben (now twelve) understands my being Gay and my relationship with my lover David. Joey (eight) still doesn't get it. He occasionally asks if David ever plans to marry. After all, his dad is Gay and he was married. If asked, he will unabashedly tell you his dad is Gay and that it's O.K. David and I are affectionate and he has slept over and vacationed with us, but Joey still doesn't know the depth of the meaning of being Gay.

Peer pressure and probable difficult situations for the boys are concerns. We have encountered some problems in this area for Ben. I try to keep avenues open for him to talk with us. Recently David and I were planning to attend the Valentine's breakfast at the boys' school, a father-sponsored function. I found out through my ex-wife that Ben was upset. It was a difficult time, but it provided an opportunity for David, Ben and me to talk. Ben didn't want us to attend together, and if we did he was going to stay home. David and I wanted to respect his feelings but didn't want to set a pattern of Ben's controlling what we do as a couple or family. Ben didn't want to hurt

46

David's feelings by not wanting him there. Ben also has some fears about his coming school years being miserable because of peer ridicule. His mother wants to protect him from that possibility.

Central to our discussion was that David and I are out. We realize there are risks and we are mostly ready to accept those risks. For Ben and Joey this will mean that peers will know their dad is Gay. It is not possible for us to protect them from that reality any more than we can protect them from the reality of their blood disorder. The teasing and social pressure brought on as a result of my (our) being Gay is unfortunate. We wish it wouldn't happen, but it probably will. There are difficulties in life that we all must deal with, and this will be a difficulty for Ben and Joey. We can offer love, help and support to cope with the problems.

In this year's parent-teacher conference, Ben's teacher described him as being self-assured and directed, popular among many but dependent on none for his identity. I could not have been more pleased. If my being Gay has prompted him to rely on himself and family for his well-being, he will grow to be a content, self-assured person. I hope Joey will do the same.

Each new perspective I have gained in life has brought me understanding and compassion for others and I hope some wisdom. My being openly Gay provides a perspective on life that benefits my children. Those benefits may be hard fought. Much in my life I have gained through struggles. The relationship I have had with my children throughout the torturing trials of their illness has given us

47

special perspectives on life. My being Gay and open with them adds to the struggle, but it also adds to the special relationship I share with Ben and Joey.

Ben has been healthy since the awful summer of '82. Joey was seriously ill for four months in 1986. After surgery and prolonged intravenous antibiotic therapy at home, he recovered and has been well since. He did not miss one day of school last year! In August of '88, we just from Washington, D.C. and a visit to the National Institute of Health, where Ben and Joey are going to participate in a study that holds exciting possibilities for improving their long-term prognosis.

Several weeks ago on their way home from school with one of Ben's sixth-grade friends, Joey calmly discussed both his mom's *and* his dad's "boy-friends." As related to me, Ben was mortified. After verifying what had been said, Ben's friend assured him that it didn't matter. We are all relieved that Ben's first open discussion with a friend about his Gay dad went so well. We look to a brightening future.

THE DAWN OF JULIE
B. Victoria Cossette

My first visit with my daughter Julie was exciting and exhausting. It was a love renewed that had been shelved for 27 years. She is five feet four, fair skinned, with short curly brown hair. Her personality is a breath of fresh air. She is quick-witted and beautiful. It startled me that we look so much alike. The most striking aspects of her visage are unquestionably the ones she inherited from me, especially her laugh! Yet only four months ago I didn't know her.

October 1986

It started with a phone call from my sister, Debbie, in Minneapolis. She said an unidentified someone had called some of our relatives trying to locate me. The word got back to Debbie, and she asked me if it was an old bill collector. I told her I had left Minneapolis 10 years ago with no bills left unpaid. But I had a feeling I knew who it was. I asked Debbie if she remembered the child I had given up for adoption twenty-seven years ago. We talked about feelings and memories that had long ago been packed away.

A month later I received a registered letter from Winona, Minnesota. Winona was the town where the adoption had taken place. I was terrified and relieved all at once — terrified because I didn't know what to expect and the guilt feelings of the adoption still haunted me, and relieved because I knew my daughter was alive and interested in finding me.

The letter said the agency was acting on my birth daughter's behalf and asked if I wanted her to know my whereabouts, also stating that correspondence and possibly a meeting could take place later. I had so many mixed emotions about that period in my life that I didn't know if I could handle this. There were questions I would not be comfortable with; and yet I wanted the meeting to take place. My employment was up in the air, as our government funding had been cut and our whole office staff would be out looking for new jobs. My life was in a rather topsy-turvy state. Still, it took me only one day to answer the registered letter. I wanted to correspond with "Dawn" (that is what I had named my little girl

27 years ago). I was cautious and chose my words carefully, not knowing why, after all these years, she would want to find me. I had never pursued a search for her because I felt I had nothing to offer and did not want to upset her life after so many years.

November 1986

I have just returned from visiting my oldest daughter Linda and her children in California. While there, I showed Linda the letter I had received from the agency. She was eager for more information and very happy, as this is her only full-blooded sister. As I looked through the mail that had piled up while I was away, I found the postmark of Winona, MN. I eagerly opened the letter and read the salutation: "Dear Mother." I'm a little in shock. I guess I never expected her to call me Mother. I cried and read on. It was a nice letter, full of information about her life. (We could not use names or cities until the agency felt our correspondence was secure.) She wrote that she was married, had a six-year-old son, and lived in a small farming community. She told of her upbringing in the area where she lives and of her adoptive family. She signed the letter, "your daughter." I wanted to answer right away as I didn't know how long ago she had sent the letter. It was hard for me to write, since I didn't know her name and felt I should not use "daughter." I decided to use "Womyn Child." I wanted my feminist awareness to come across because I wanted her to know my values. I told her of my involvement with my organizations, my job and my home life. I told her I shared my home with her two half-sisters and a "roommate." I decided to sign the letter "Your Birth Mother." I was comfortable with that.

December 1986

Another letter passed between us and then she enclosed a picture. The picture was lovely. It was a family picture of her husband, her son and herself. When I looked at her in the picture, it was like looking at a photo of myself twenty years ago. I had goose-bumps and could not take my eyes off it. Another realization finally sank in: this was the baby I gave up for adoption — she was real, she was a grown woman, an extension of myself. I had wanted her to have everything I couldn't give her. Love was the only thing I could offer now.

Seeing the picture hurt more than I can say. It brought to the surface the love I've always had but was afraid to feel. Why did the pain that I felt so many years ago feel ten times worse now? Couldn't I have raised another child? She was no different than the other children, and yet she was very different: I gave her up. I had to think back . . . the reasons didn't seem so important now.

She asked me to send her a picture of myself in my next letter. Luckily, I had just had a professional picture taken. I enclosed it and waited for her response. The next letter that came had her name and return address on it. Her name is *Julie,* and she lives in Good Thunder, Minnesota. She said it was so wonderful to finally see someone that she looked like. I guess I had never thought of that; it's something you take for granted. She enclosed her telephone number and asked if I would call soon. She wanted to come to Florida and meet me and her siblings.

I called Julie that evening. I was scared to death, and it took three tries to complete the call. I was having one hot flash after another!! We talked for a long time. She described her childhood, her family and her son. She asked questions about her brothers and sisters and about other family members, but not the one I expected — WHY. We had a good talk and the ice was broken. She sounded great, she had her life together and everything was going well for her. She mentioned that she wanted to visit at Christmas time. I decided that it would be too hectic for a visit at that time of year and suggested January. We discussed her travel plans. I knew then that I had to tell her about my lifestyle.

When I decided to go to an adoption agency 27 years ago I went to the Catholic Welfare Agency, knowing that they screened the adoptive parents well and that my child would be in a stable home. I figured she had been raised Catholic (the pattern of perfection drummed into her for 27 years) and would probably have very strong convictions on homosexuality. (Since that time, my beliefs have changed drastically.)

I took a deep breath and tried to slide the truth past, barely finishing one sentence and quickly adding "I have to mention that I live an alternative lifestyle." I waited, probably 3 seconds (but forever), and she said, "Exactly what is an alternative lifestyle?"

How do you (carefully) tell someone you've never met, who means a great deal to you, that you are a lesbian? I felt I owed her the truth. I didn't want her to arrive here alone and have the fact dumped on her, with no support system of her own. I simply blurted out the truth. Her response was refreshingly mature. She stated it was fine with her whatever I was, as she was interested in finally meeting me after all those years, and it didn't bother her at all. Could I expect anything less from my own daughter?

Now I didn't tell her that one daughter was also a lesbian and that my "roommate" was my lover. I would save that for later.

January 1987

She arrived at 11:30 a.m. on January 14. I dressed conservatively (for me), remembering that the dictionary definition of lesbian was "mannish female" and wanting Julie to meet her birth mother, not her birth father. As my lover Bekah and I were on our way to the airport, I stopped at our local florist to pick up a single yellow rose to give to her. The yellow rose signified my mother's presence with me, who is the driving force in my life. I had made a large sign saying "WELCOME JULIE." Of course, just when you think you've got this all down right, something happens like the plane being 45 minutes late. I paced, had hot flashes, and smoked one cigarette after another. I WAS AN EXPECTANT MOTHER.

As the plane pulled up to the gate, I was right up front, Bekah by my side, anxiously awaiting Julie's arrival into our twilight zone. Then the crowd of people gathered in and we got pushed to the middle.

Three million people come to Florida in January to claim the Sun God in the temple on the beach with suntan lotion in hand, and the airplane was jammed. But I spotted Julie immediately, raised my sign up in the air and shouted "Julie, Julie." She smiled and we found each other in the crowd, hugged and held on for quite a while. Bekah took a few pictures, and I introduced them. Julie was smaller than I had pictured, but far prettier than in the photo. My heart must have been beating a mile a minute. I stumbled for the right words, but basic stupid came out.

We went to pick up her luggage, and while waiting we talked about her flight, her family and the weather. I wanted to grab her, hold on, tell her I was sorry, tell her I loved her and had never stopped loving her. But my fear took over and I was held back.

When we arrived home I didn't know where to begin. I know she was feeling the same uneasiness I was; I could tell by her conversation. I gave her the ten-cent tour of the house and shared some of my feelings about her anticipated arrival. She was able to joke about a lot of the surrounding circumstances, which broke the ice.

When Tany and Tiffany (her half-sisters) arrived home from work, they immediately broke through our nervousness as they told some of the family secrets. They both had a difficult time saying "Mom" instead of "my mom" when talking about me. They both liked her and were impressed. She fit right in . . . she was finally home. They started showing her pictures of the rest of the family. You know the kind, brothers with missing teeth and home haircuts, aunts that look a hundred pounds lighter, me in a bee-hive hairdo with a blow-up bra that made Dolly Parton look like a triple A. The laughter was good.

Then Julie gave me her gift, an album she had put together of her growing up years. There were baby pictures (when her adoptive parents first saw her), family, school, graduation and wedding pictures. She was gorgeous in her white wedding gown. I cried and felt overwhelmed with feelings that I didn't know how to express. I realized she was given all the opportunities I prayed she would have — love, health, a stable family, a good home life, education, a good marriage and a family.

We had a small dinner party where she met her brother Gary and they became acquainted. Also, it was at this time that Julie and Bekah became very close. They discussed my lesbianism and Bekah's role as my mate. Julie said our lifestyle didn't bother her at all. She said she was impressed by the love and nurturing that we all had for one another, and she was glad to finally meet her mother and find out about her brothers and sisters. She told Bekah that she was glad her mother had such a wonderful womyn in her life.

When we had a chance to talk alone about the circumstances of her adoption, I told her that I had been divorced from her father. At the time of the adoption I was 20 years old with three children at home. I was an abused spouse, married at only 15 and having babies one after the other. Her father was a brutal person who raped me just six weeks after her brother Gary had been born, and as a result she was conceived. I was broken in spirit and body, and when I learned I was pregnant again, the only thing I

56

could think about was taking my life. I felt I couldn't raise another baby; I believed I couldn't escape from my abusive husband. My chance came when he was put in jail. He'd been arrested after almost killing Gary. After gathering my thoughts and my children, I went alone to Austin, Minnesota, where I healed (physically and spiritually) and gave birth to Julie. It was here, in safety at last, that I decided to give her up for adoption. I wanted a family to raise her and give her the love and time I could not. After revealing all this to Julie, I believe she knew that in my heart I only gave her up so she could have what I couldn't give her. It was difficult to dig into the memories and lay myself out for judgment, but I wanted Julie to know the WHY.

On Saturday we had a little party at our local coffee house, Joffrey's. Several of our lesbian and gay male friends came to meet the new addition; I should have passed out cigars. There were about 16 friends, all wanting to welcome Julie. Her reaction to our friends was very warm and accepting. Afterwards we decided to take Julie to one of our local womyn's bars. We all got on the dance floor at once and danced in a womyn's circle. Then Bekah had the DJ play "We Are Family." I felt wonderful! Julie had accepted my love, my lifestyle, and my friends.

She joked that the Catholic Welfare Agencies had charged her $270.00 for locating me. This entailed two long distance phone calls, one registered letter, and a few office visits. She kept saying, "Was it worth it to pay all that for this crazy family?"

Sunday came too soon. We still had a lifetime to catch up on. I felt sad knowing in just a few hours I had to take her to the airport, and I didn't know

when I would see her again. We became
mother/daughter and friends in just a few short days.

The family all went to the airport. It was some
kind of wonderful, and so sad too. We waited as they
announced the flight to Minnesota. We each took our
turn, and hugged and cried and told Julie to come
back soon with her family next time. My turn was
last and the tears were flowing freely now. I hugged
her, kissed her, and didn't want to let go. I thanked
her for the courage to find me and for the special
person she had become. The heaviness in my heart
was like the good-bye 27 years ago. But now I know
where she is and *who* she is. And she knows who I
am.

April 1987

It took three months to get my feelings down on
paper. As I sit here writing, I reminisce about
everything that happened. I am thinking how lucky I
am to have a daughter like Julie. She is back in
Minnesota, I am back carrying on with my life. We
write and stay in touch. I look forward to the day
when we can be together again. Our relationship will
flourish; *we are family.*

COMING OUT TO BRIAN
Fred Flotho
Edited by Loralee MacPike

Everyone else in the family had known that I was gay for several years, but I had not told Brian. But at last I knew that the time had come when I could no longer continue to hide from him.

Brian is developmentally disabled, a term that I don't think I had ever fully faced until I wrote it in this sentence. I have never believed that he is retarded; he has a serious communication problem because of the extreme doses of anti-convulsant drugs that he must take in an attempt to control his seizure disorder, and his speech is consequently slurred to the point that even with a great deal of practice, we have to give 100% attention to his efforts and even then must extrapolate meaning without understanding all his words. But when he communicates, it is clear from his responses that he understands what is being said to him and thinks productively about it before answering. When he can express himself verbally, it is also evident that he has a wonderful memory not only for current happenings but also for things that happened when he was a child. His brain works perfectly well. But his ability to relate its workings verbally is impaired to the point that there is no way to know what is stored in that brain. And so it was with trepidation that I approached the issue of coming out to Brian.

Until he was twenty-six, I had simply avoided the issue. My position had been supported by his psychologist and others working with him in his current living situation, in which he got a lot of help toward eventually living independently. The only one opposing my position was my wife.

After three years of trying to work out an acceptable life with my wife for me as a gay man, I gave up. I was just not able to live a lie in the closet any more. I decided I had to be me — but that meant that I could no longer hide from Brian if I was not living with his mother. Up to this point, almost all of my coming-out experiences had been positive, even wonderful, in that most often I found a greater acceptance than I had dreamed possible. My relationships with a number of my non-gay friends had become much deeper once they knew I was gay, and I think this was because I was more open, more knowable, than I had been when I was in the closet.

I could only hope that telling Brian would have the same result.

The day came when Brian came home for the weekend, and the three of us were gathered around the breakfast table. The first bomb: "Brian, your mother and I are separating."

Brian's response came with greater clarity than I usually hear from him. "Well, dad and mom, you've always been great parents to me and have supported me through all the hard times I've had, and I love you both the same as I always have." Brian saw the tears come to my eyes for the first time; I had just learned how to cry.

The next bomb: "Brian, the reason we're separating is that I'm gay."

"Gee, dad, that's all right. I have a friend who's gay, and he's told me how hard it is for him." I have never been sure what his friend's difficulties were, but it really didn't make any difference at that moment. Brian understood what I had been saying, and it was all right with him! He had no fear, and his fearlessness erased my own fear. I was still the same dad to Brian that I had been for his 26 years, and that would never change.

"Brian, neither of us is going to abandon you. We'll still be here when you need us. It's just that we won't be living in the same house any more."

"Gee, dad, I knew that." At this point, I had run out of words but Brian hadn't run out of thoughts. He came around the table and gave his mom a big hug and they cried for a minute. I was next.

Now, Brian's two brothers know I am gay and have always been very supportive, and their support and love are immensely important to me. But the thoughts coming out of Brian's mouth so clearly that day were what I had most wanted, and what I had most feared I would never have.

Brian usually calls home about once a week to report on how things are going. The week after my coming-out, he called me at my new home. "Dad, I just wanted to call to find out how you were doing." And after some routine conversation, he added, "I have some good news — I'm going to graduate from Project Independence in September. They think I'm ready to live independently!" He apparently didn't even skip a beat, but my heart burst with pride for this open, gentle, loving young man who has been so dear to me. How could I ever have considered not coming out to him? I know now what's really important in my life.

WHO I AM
Josephine d'Antonio

If only I could tell you who I am. This whole issue of being a lesbian. To make you understand in words your age level permits. How do I explain that what you see on television news briefs (like men in women's makeup and dresses, or women in men's clothes) is not what your mom is all about? In my limited way I shall try, because it is more important for you to hear this from me than from a lawyer in court or one of your friends in school.

You were raised with one mom and one dad. Dad taught classes at the Community College, and I enjoyed staying home and raising the three of you. I loved it. I loved baking cookies and listening to you all run into the kitchen after school and give me a big hug. You realized at a young age how very much daddy and I adored each of you. You felt our love, always and first. Who I am today could never change any of that. It can never fade or be taken away.

You also saw me doing things your friends' moms didn't do, like changing the oil in our cars or putting up wallpaper better than dad did. I enjoyed these things as much as getting all dressed up special for your dad and going dancing for the evening. Sometimes I felt feminine, sometimes masculine. I, like you, had different parts to my personality. Even though I did masculine things sometimes, it didn't mean I was unhappy being a woman.

Somewhere around the age of 35 I realized I needed more for me. Up to this point, my life had often felt like someone else was living it. I did what was expected of me for my parents first, then for your dad, for my church, and yes, even for you guys too. But that wasn't completely me. I'm not saying it was all a terrible life by most standards. My mother thought that I had done quite well for myself. I was respected as dad's wife at the College and a real good mom to your friends. But inside I carried a sadness I couldn't hide any more.

You all saw a terrible time in our life which lasted two years. Our picture-perfect family was falling apart. *I* was falling apart. I didn't tell anyone how lonely I was feeling. Oh, I tried to tell dad, but he was always too busy at the College, or going to classes for another degree, or involved in his church activities. Dad and I were never in love, just friends. We weren't even best friends. We lived like two strangers putting in time. We drained each other. Finally I moved out of our bedroom and began to drink heavily and take pills to be peppy and pills to sleep. For two years you had a zombie mom too weak and frightened to do anything about her life. To my dying day I shall regret the lost energy and the damage I allowed to come between us.

As I reflect on it all today, I can only say once again that I was very, very sick, and people who are sick don't always do the right thing. Dad would not give me a divorce and I couldn't face leaving you kids to him. So I drank and tried to forget how unhappy I felt.

It took me two years to realize it was you three I was hurting the most — and that was what I most wanted *not* to do. I needed someone to talk to, to share things with, to love and be loved in return. I was always raised to believe a woman didn't have "special women friends" outside of one's own family members. I felt strange around other women; I felt I liked them too much.

After a great deal of therapy, I met someone who made me feel very special. This was Mrs. M. We talked and laughed, cried and did all the wonderful things I longed to do with another person — things dad and I never did. I was like a sponge soaking it all up. I fell in love with her. We shared many years together, but she got very sick and died of cancer. I had lost my best and special friend.

Her dying taught me something. It taught me I am lovable, and I can love again. I needed to be in love. But I also learned I couldn't live with dad any more. I wanted to live with my lover. I wanted to live as a happy family again and do things with all of you. I lost everything in the divorce except you three, but to me that was the greatest victory I could have won. We were poorer, but we could all laugh together.

When I met Tesa we decided after a year to live together and raise you kids as ours. She took to you so quickly, and you knew that the respect of two people with a goal was most important to us all. I explained to you that we were lesbians and that loving each other was no different than a dad and mom loving each other. We were just the same sex. I told you that you were not loved less, and that if things didn't work out I wanted to hear this from you. You understood somehow and were eager for Tesa to live with us. I loved you the more for understanding and loving her too.

I guess in my heart I knew you would accept my decision, but I did have a tremendous fear of your not. That fear came to light when your older brother told us he wanted to move in with dad. He felt he could not accept my new lifestyle and moved out. I accepted his decision and loved him for being so honest with his feelings.

EPILOGUE: Two of you stayed with us. We share a beautiful life again. We laugh, go on long weekends, love and respect each other. For this I will be forever a proud mom.

G-STRINGS FOR DADDY
Elliott A. Brager

I separated from my wife in January 1980 at a time when my son was 10 and my daughter was 8. I felt that they were too young then to understand the real reason why Mommy and Daddy would not be living together any more. All they knew was that Mommy and Daddy argued a lot, but they didn't really understand the subject matter of our arguments; so I waited for a time that I thought was best for them.

I waited until a month after my son's Bar Mitzvah in August 1982, and I decided to tell them then. I also decided to tell them separately, which was a wise decision for me. I told my daughter Laurie first. She was 11 then. She asked all the questions I would expect an inquiring child to ask: Did I know I was gay when I met Mommy? Did I know I was gay when I got married? Did I kiss men? Did I dance with men? She seemed to be more curious and more understanding.

My son, on the other hand, I think, perceived it to be a slight threat to him. He burst into tears; he was very unhappy. He didn't want to discuss it any further. We took a ride, and after an hour he started asking me questions: was this particular friend of mine gay, was this one gay, was that one gay? He was going down the list of all the friends of mine that he knew. Finally, I reached a point that I told him, "Barry, if you want to know if they're gay, ask them yourself."

There came a point when I finally knew that my children accepted my gayness. In October 1982, which was only two months after I told them, my wife's younger sister was turning 30, and her husband was throwing a surprise 30th birthday party for her, to which, of course, I was not invited; but I knew my wife and children would be going. On that particular Sunday night I was out. When I came home, there were two excited messages on my answering machine — one from my son and one from my daughter — encouraging me to return their calls. It was too late that night, but the next morning I called. I reached my daughter first. The thing that they both were so anxious to tell me was that the surprise for my sister-in-law was a male dancer who stripped down to a G-string. Both my children were excited to tell me how good-looking he was and how much I would have enjoyed it!

As for problems that my gayness has created between my children and me, I simply haven't had any. Of course, we have problems, but they're because I'm daddy and they're teenagers, and those are the sort of problems I'm happy to have, because they are symbols of the very real parent-child relationship I have with my children. So many divorced fathers, especially gay ones who don't come out to their children, drift out of the children's lives and end up losing their children emotionally forever. I've discovered that if you're not so hot as a husband, you ought to try to be the best darned father you can be, or someone else will come along to father those children, and it will be too late. Lovers come and lovers go, but your children are always your children.

Since telling Barry and Laurie, I have been active and visible in fundraising for the Gay and Lesbian Community Center of Baltimore. Both children are accustomed to my visibility and very comfortable with my gay friends in gay settings. However, the value of our open relationship was really brought home to me in September 1988, when I participated in selling tickets to Baltimore's first major AIDS fundraising event. At the function, approximately 60% of the contributor/participants were straight. For her seventeenth birthday present, I bought Laurie a sophisticated new party dress and an orchestra seat next to me and some of my gay friends for the concert; afterwards, I escorted her to a gay disco where we danced — and she didn't want to leave! She spent her first whole evening with straight people who knew her father was gay — a very different kind of situation than the usual accepting crowd of fellow gays — without the least self-consciousness. I know she's as proud of me as I am of her. And me — well, telling my children was the best thing I could have done for them *and* for myself.

Adapted from an article in *The Baltimore Gay paper*, June 1987, Baltimore, MD; by permission of *The Baltimore Gaypaper*.

III
THE PROCESS
OF COMING OUT

For many gay and Lesbian parents, coming out is a process, less like a slide flashed onto a screen and more like the assembly of a complex jigsaw puzzle, taking shape slowly as the picture emerges from an originally confusing array of tiny insights and glimpses. And even when coming out takes the form of an announcement, the reality of our Lesbian and gay lives is fully revealed only as they are lived out, by us and by our children. The *process* of coming out to our children is therefore a daily experience, a growth of understanding, an accretion of events and feelings, an ongoing disclosure on our part, acknowledgement on theirs — acknowledgement which often leads to acceptance. Movement forward toward acceptance may be slow, and at times it may not even be visible to us; but without the disclosure of ourselves which initiates the process of coming-out, no movement is possible.

THE MOTHER FROM OUTER SPACE
Betty Mansfield

It happened to be Gay Pride Day, '87. It happened to be the week before her ninth birthday. And we happened to have the whole day to ourselves, since my younger daughter was at a party. That was the day I told my older daughter that I am a lesbian. And that day stands in my mind as one of the most fulfilling days of my life: when, to my surprise, *I* learned who *she* was and who she was growing up to be.

* * * * *

When I first started to come to grips with the fact that my marriage was not worth saving, I went to counseling. I'd had casual affairs with two women and I needed to find out if the attraction that I felt to women was worth risking my family over. At that time, I still lived with Matt, but we were both very unhappy. He drank a lot. We fought a lot. We felt bitter and angry and resentful. And neither of us wanted to destroy the family (what, in fact, our friends thought was "the perfect family").

The counseling helped tremendously. It helped me to realize that I might never again be "the happy wife," but I could be happy with myself. I could be honest with myself, but (I had to ask myself) could I be honest with my daughters? I could adjust, but could they?

One of the things I realized then was that I did not need to announce my sexual preferences to the whole world. It was not everyone's business. But if I wanted to feel good about myself, that meant being honest with those who were close to me, including my daughters. So I decided that I would tell them the truth — as soon as they were old enough to keep a secret.

The three years between my leaving Matt and my coming out to Julie were chaotic ones for us all. At first I lived in an apartment with my female "roommate." I saw the girls three or four times a week, and once a week they would sleep over with me. Every few months Matt would have to go out of town on business, and then I would move into the house for a two- or three-week period. I didn't like

74

the fact that Matt's standard of living was higher than mine, and sometimes I missed Julie and Lisa running into my room every morning with hugs and kisses, and sometimes I felt guilty for not being there, especially when Matt was drinking. But at the time, it seemed like the only way to work things out. Besides, I had a woman I loved, and I loved sleeping with her, something I was not going to deny myself any more.

Still, I could not imagine living with her and the kids under one roof. Matt had refused to move from the house, and I could not afford to live there on my own. And I dreaded the thought of a custody battle. Who would the court sympathize with — a parent who had a drinking problem (as so many do) or one who was gay (as so few will admit)?

Then Matt got drunk one night and ran his car into a telephone pole. He hasn't had a drink since then, and I now feel better about entrusting him with Julie and Lisa. But my lover and I split up too, and once again I could not afford a place of my own. At first I tried living at the house with the kids — Matt slept downstairs — but I soon realized I had to live apart from him. Soon after I moved into my new apartment, Jean moved in. Julie and Lisa liked her, and Matt and I tried our best to be friends. After all, we both wanted the same thing: to do what was best for the children. We began divorce mediation.

It was at divorce mediation that I brought up the idea of my coming out to Julie. Matt said he didn't think it was a good idea.

"Why not?" I asked.

"Well, because I can't imagine how to say something like that without making it sound bad."

"Well, I can't imagine saying it so that it *does* sound bad," I countered.

"Then I think you should be the one to tell her."

That acknowledgement had come much more easily than I had expected. Whether he would have come to that decision without the mediators in the room is doubtful. But I was glad to hear the words come from his mouth. I had always thought the issue with Matt was whether or not Julie should be told, not who was to tell her.

It was, after all, my right to be the one to tell her. And I would have told her anyway, but I wanted him to agree because I sincerely want him to understand, eventually, that my being gay is not a bad thing.

Anyway, he is an adult. Whether or not *he'll* ever understand is of no great or immediate importance, though it would be nice. But would *she* understand? Or would she already have heard so many anti-gay jokes that she'd think me laughable? Would she, by now, have picked up the hateful tones that even children use when they say "gay"? Would she hate me? Would my telling her confirm some suspicion she already had and would this be a harsh settling-in of reality? Would she be disappointed? Would she be embarrassed? Might it seem to her that her dad was right after all, and mom was wrong?

Regardless of my fears, the day of reckoning had come.

As I said before, it was Gay Pride Day, '87. In New York City, there was a parade. I'd been there

76

the year before with my ex-lover. I recalled all the positive energy that had prevailed there, all that unity and pride and optimism. Now, a year later, I felt some of that energy again and it gave me some courage.

Julie and I had the day to ourselves, a warm and pleasant afternoon with no particular plans besides talking and having lunch. We were driving around and talking about where to eat. She wanted nachos. I drove toward the Tastee Freez and felt myself getting nervous at the thought of telling her. But I plunged in. Or waded in, I suppose.

"I'm glad we have this time together." *God, I sound like Carol Burnett!* I thought.

"Yeah, me too."

"There's something I want to talk to you about."

"What?"

"Well. There's something I want to tell you about me . . . It's nothing bad. I just want you to know, because I want you to know me."

She laughed. "Of course I know you. You're my mother."

I laughed too, out of nervousness. "Well, yes, you do know me pretty well, huh? You know what I like and what I do at work and who my friends are and what makes me angry . . . but there's something else. How about the Tastee Freez? They usually have pretty good nachos."

"Sure."

We got there and ordered our food and sat in the car eating. My stomach was in knots. "Let's just eat first and then we'll talk, okay?"

We ate, then I meticulously wrapped up the trash. "Let me just get rid of this now . . ."

77

I tossed the trash and got back into the car. She looked at me. "What do you want to tell me?"

"Well, I'm really nervous about telling you . . . I hope you won't hate me or . . . Maybe you already know . . ."

"What?"

I took a deep breath. "You know what gay means, right?" (We'd talked about the word before, a word which, I discovered, they use at school the way "queer" was used when I was in grade school, to mean silly or out of style as well as homosexual.)

"Yeah, it means like when a man loves another man and they kiss and, you know, have sex. Why? What about it?"

"Well, I'm gay."

She looked at me as if I'd suddenly put on a funny hat. "That's lesbian," she said flatly.

"Well, okay, I'm lesbian."

"With who?" she asked, with the same incredulous look.

"With Jean."

"Why?"

"Well, because I love her. Because after a long time of being with your dad, things weren't that good any more and I decided to try being with a woman. I guess I always wanted to, but I loved Daddy, so I didn't see anybody else. But then I was with a woman and I found out I liked it."

"Is that why you and Daddy got separated?"

"That was one of the reasons. We had a lot of trouble and neither of us was very happy. You remember how Daddy used to drink."

"Yeah. And you were fighting all the time. It is

78

better now that you don't live with each other. . . .
Do you and Jean sleep together?"

"Yes. But you know that this has to be a secret,
right? You can't tell anyone, even Lisa. As far as
she's concerned, I sleep in the other room and pull
out the sofa bed each night."

"Oh, I know! Especially Lisa! She'd blab, like she
did at Christmas. Don't worry."

"Yeah. And you have to remember that some
people think it's really a bad thing to be gay, or
lesbian. They think it means you're a bad person."

"I know. There were two lesbians in my class last
year and lots of kids made fun of them, but I didn't."

"In the third grade??"

"Yeah, Jane and Elizabeth. You could just tell.
They were always together and always wanting to
hug and kiss and people could tell."

"And they made fun of them?"

"Yeah, but I didn't."

"That's good."

"Well, I figure it's not really my business if they
want to be that way."

"Yeah," I said, totally amazed at this point by
how well the conversation was going. It was one of
those times, which I guess all parents experience,
when you look at your child and realize that old
cliche: *my, how fast they grow up!*

"So, you don't think there's anything wrong with
being gay? Or do you?" I asked.

"No," she answered thoughtfully. "I don't think it
makes much difference. I think the most important
thing is that you love somebody."

"Yeah?"

79

"Yeah, like this girl in my class, Jennifer, she's in love with Jeremy and he's in a wheelchair. A lot of the girls make fun of her, but I don't think it's a bad thing at all. He's one of the smartest and nicest boys in the school, and if she loves him, I think it's good."

I looked at her again, this kid I thought I knew so well. She looked so grown up, her little blonde eyebrows drawn toward each other, her blue eyes searching for the right words as she spoke. And there in the parking lot of the Tastee Freez, I felt my love for her growing, my pride in her greater than ever, and I felt my life beginning to change.

"You know, you are one hell of a smart kid. I'm so proud of you."

"Thanks," she said.

I gave her a hug and said, "Let's go for a ride."

As we headed up the road and through the park, I felt my whole body relax. "You know," I said, "I just gave you some pretty big news and you don't seem very surprised. Did you know already?"

"Well, I thought there was something a little fishy, but I wasn't sure what."

"What made you suspicious?"

"Well, I saw something at your apartment that said 'lesbian' on it, some book that was on your bookshelf. It's not there any more. Plus, you're always with Jean and sometimes you just seem like more than friends, you know?"

"Yeah. Well, so you think being gay is okay and everything, but how do you feel about your own mother being gay? I want you to be honest, okay? And I won't be hurt or anything. I want to know how you feel about it."

"Well," she hedged a little. "It's a little like having a mother from outer space."

"What? Does it seem that weird to you?"

"No, no. I don't think it's *weird*. It's just . . . unusual."

"Well, yes, it's not the usual thing, that's true. You don't see much about it in movies unless they're making fun of it, but it's not as unusual as you might think, either. I know lots of women who are lesbians, and some of them have kids too."

"Really? Who?"

"Somebody named Judy that you never met. She has a little girl who's two and a half. Her name is Sandy. They live with another lesbian friend who's not her lover but who helps with parenting."

"I'd like to meet them."

And so the conversation went for a while. We rode around and talked. Julie was amazed to find out that my brother, Bob, was gay too, and that many of my friends she'd met were lesbians. She was also surprised that those women didn't look "like guys."

"I thought that to be lesbian you had to sort of dress like a guy and have short hair and all that. That's why I wasn't too sure about you. You don't look like that."

"No. A lot of people think that way, but lesbians just dress and act the way they feel comfortable. For some, that means jeans and a T-shirt most of the time, but others feel just as comfortable with a skirt and heels. Linda is a lesbian, and so is T.J."

"Wow, really? T.J. dresses so cool!"

"Yeah, I dated T.J. for a while."

"You did? She's cute! Who else did you date?"

And so we chatted away about who dated whom,

81

and Julie smiled and leaned forward, feeling very grown up to be in on this secret. And then there was a nice, comfortable silence as we rode and finally I said, "You know, I'm relieved that I finally told you about this. I hated keeping a secret from you for so long."

"How long was it?"

"About three years."

She pondered this. "So, was Barbara your girlfriend too? Before Jean?"

"Yeah."

"I liked her too. I miss her sometimes."

"Yeah, she was nice."

"That *was* a long time."

"Yes, it was. I'm glad it's out in the open now. Between you and me, anyway."

"Me too. Now I feel like I can talk more about my feelings, too. Like if I have something to tell you, you'll listen and not think I'm weird."

"That's right, sweetie. Just like you've listened to me. I'm your friend."

"You know, something happened to me last year at school and I've been kind of worried about it."

"What happened?"

"Well, one time Sara gave me a really big hug and kiss, and I liked it."

"It seems pretty natural that you would like a big hug and kiss from your best friend."

"But it was more than just that . . . it felt weird. It was like when she kissed me I felt like I was a boy. I was really worried that maybe I'm a lesbian, but mostly I like boys and think about them. Mostly I like Todd."

"Most people do like both men and women, at

least a little bit. But they don't admit it. They try to pretend it's not so. That's because they think you have to be either gay or straight. What they don't realize is that you don't have to like just one sex or the other. Especially when you're growing up, it's very normal to have those kinds of attractions to the same sex. It doesn't mean you'll be a lesbian."

"You don't think I'm a lesbian?"

"I don't think you have to decide that for a long, long time. And just because your mother is a lesbian doesn't mean you'll be one. You just take things as they come and figure it out as you go along."

"I really do love Todd, still. He's the cutest and nicest and smartest boy I've ever known."

"He's lucky that you feel that way. And if you ever want to talk about sex, about feelings you have about boys or girls, you know who you can talk to."

"Yeah. You." We smiled at each other.

"And you don't have to feel like a daughter from outer space." We laughed.

It's Mother's Day, 1988. Julie and Lisa are sleeping in the next room, so I'm writing this by hand. I've re-read the story and I'm thinking what the reader is probably thinking now: This all sounds made up. Yet it's true, almost word for word. I'm also thinking: There's no story here because there's no conflict. It all went so well that day. Yet so much has happened since then.

Since that dreaded, happy day, so many Problems that I feared never came to be. And most of the Problems That Are are not problems of a parent coming out, but of a family coming apart. It's never easy.

Here are two children who seem very well-adjusted, though at times, I'm sure, they'd rather have a "normal" family. Lisa still doesn't know her mom is gay. Julie, who bites her lip when the kids at school make fun of gays, sometimes wishes her mom were straight, "just because it's easier to be normal." Easier for some.

Here are two parents who have always tried to do what is right, one who has struggled to be truthful, and one who, I'm sure, feels he's been lied to. I hope someday he'll understand. But anyway, we're friends.

It's hard for me to judge the difficulties that my children might be facing. They seem so well-accustomed to the back-packing over to Mom's and the packing back to Dad's. Me, I grew up in an unhappy home and I feel glad that my children have something I never had: parents who are (finally) at peace with themselves.

Let me try to describe how things have changed since the day I came out to Julie, and how, in many ways, I've become a stronger person.

In October of 1987 Jean and I went to the March on Washington for Gay Rights. We rode down on a bus with several other gay men and women, some of whom we knew, some whom we'd just met. Yet, we were all like family. When we arrived, we met up with about 300 other marchers from Akron. The spirit there was one of strength and unity and determination and — more than ever before — of sadness.

At the front of the March that day were hundreds of PWA's (persons with AIDS). One of those PWA's chose to wait up for his friends from Akron. He chose to stand around in the cold while it threatened to rain because he knew his sister would be there to walk with him, too. That man was my brother Bob.

Bob is ten years younger than I am, but in many ways he's been like a big brother. He had the guts to come out long before I did. For a while I was afraid to admit to Bob my own gayness. I felt it was different in my case. After all, I had a family, a responsibility. Bob was single and free to live as he chose. I thought he would disrespect me or sympathize more with Matt or hate me for not having come out sooner. On the contrary, he'd already guessed. "I was waiting for you to tell me," I remember him saying when I finally told him. "You should have known you could talk to me."

That was almost four years ago. More than anyone else, Bob has helped me to like myself, to be honest, to be strong. He'd listen whenever I had a crush on some woman (oh, how difficult to experience adolescence twice!) or when I felt worried or nervous or low. He helped me come out to myself. He introduced me to his friends. He took me to the bars. He loved me like a big brother does.

In June of 1986 Bob came down with AIDS. He's had two bouts of pneumocystic pneumonia but overall has done very well. It puts things in perspective, certainly. When I find myself feeling sorry for myself or going on about how hard it is — to adjust, to be a single mother, to meet women at the bars — I have to catch myself and think of Bob. He's afflicted with what's probably the most frightening disease of our time. He can't have sex at all. He can't be near children much for fear of catching some little virus

85

that would kill him. He had to quit a job that he worked hard to get. People talk behind his back, probably. He must have blood tests and medications and be cautious of any little thing . . . and probably he'll die anyway. And yet, he's strong. He doesn't feel sorry for himself. He doesn't shrink from those things he feels are his duties. He manages, with all of this, to be happy and proud and loving.

Anyhow, Bob was there when we arrived in Washington. He met some of my friends. I met some of his. We stood in the cold all morning and half the afternoon, waiting our turn to march. I threatened to "tell mommy" if he didn't put on a sweater a friend had offered him, so he did. We were milling about when I noticed three placards lying on the ground. I picked one up: it read "Lesbian Mother." *More than just a sign,* I thought, *This is a Sign.*

I carried the sign, and as I walked up Pennsylvania Avenue toward the Capitol, I watched the faces of the people who stood along the sidewalk, so many faces that lit up, hands that raised the "love" sign toward me, voices that shouted, "Yeah, lesbian mother. We love you."

A woman ran up from behind me, yelling, "Lesbian mom, where are you?" and she told me her story: She'd left her husband and taken her children and was living with another woman and now she was trying to win a very bitter custody battle. She carried the sign for a while.

One man approached me and asked incredulously, but politely, "How did *that* happen?"

A boy, a cute, healthy-looking kid of about sixteen, rushed up to me shouting wildly, "Awright! Lesbian Mother! Gimme five!" I smiled back and slapped his outstretched hand, thinking that he must be making fun of me, this punk, and he went on, "My mother's a lesbian and she's great!"

The experience of thatmarch was very affirmative for me. It helped me to see that not only is it my right to admit who I am, it is my duty. Now I realize that speaking up is not just okay, but good, good because it is the truth and because people need to hear it. Even as I write this, I'm thinking of someone who might be reading it, someone who is just as I was five years ago — feeling confused and guilty and wondering if there is anybody else in the world who has ever faced this kind of situation.

My relationship with Jean was short-lived. I met Donna in December, just before Jean moved out. She is very easy to be with, and it is a relationship that strengthens me.

Another thing that makes me feel stronger is the acceptance and support I have found in many of my co-workers since I came out to them. They are almost all women, all around my age, almost all have children, and they are for the most part a very sensitive and intelligent group of people. So I feel fortunate in that, over the three years I've worked there, I've been able to come out gradually to most of them.

Of course, initially I was very much concerned that to reveal myself might jeopardize my job. I'd come out to just two women at work before my talk with Julie. After that, for some reason, it's been easier to tell other people. I'm not sure why. It just gets easier with each person I tell. There are a few I have chosen not to tell, simply because I'm not that close to them. But for the most part, I can be myself at work. I can go into the staff lounge and talk with someone about where she went with her husband or her kids and then I can say, "Donna and I took the kids to the park." It all seems so normal; and, like Julie, I like to feel normal.

Coming out at work not only helped me feel better about myself, but I believe it raised some consciousness there about gays. One of my co-workers told me just a few weeks ago that she was glad I had trusted her, had let her in on that part of my life, finally.

"You know," she said, "I'm really glad I got to know you. And I'm really glad to know you have someone to love. If you ever get married, I want to be there."

"Sure," I joked, "maybe you can be the maid of honor or the best woman, whichever."

She laughed with me, then in a more serious tone said, "But I mean it. I think it's great that you're happy."

"You know," she went on, "I always thought I hated lesbians. But what I hated was the stereotype. You know, someone tough and crass and man-hating, what I *thought* lesbians were. I'm just glad you told me and I got to see that it's not that way. It's okay now, you know? Someone's being gay is no big deal any more."

Needless to say (but I'll say it anyway), that should give us all some hope. What I keep finding out is that people, in general, have a lot more love and understanding in them than I used to believe. And, time and time again, where I've expected scorn or criticism, I've found acceptance and understanding.

Finally, I felt brave enough to tell my parents.

They had long ago accepted Bob's homosexuality. Then they had to accept his having AIDS. As I said, that tends to put things in perspective. As it turned out, my parents had already surmised the truth. When I told my mother, her response was a gentle, "Oh, honey, I know that. That's never mattered."

In fact, not only were my parents allowing me to choose the time that I would tell them; they were already beginning to accept it. They'd known my first woman lover fairly well, and they loved her. And now I can see that they loved her not in spite of the fact that she loved me, but because she did.

Of course, there are Problems. My parents have accepted it. But because I waited so long to tell them, they had already assumed that I was the one at fault when Matt and I separated. Never mind his drinking; my mother tolerated my father's drinking for forty years. They are from the old school that teaches that tolerance is a woman's lot. Now they have a better understanding, but my father still takes it personally. So we just don't talk about it much. And, surprisingly, he is learning tolerance.

And, of course, there's still the question of when to tell Lisa. I think I'll wait, if I can, until she's about nine, since Julie accepted it so well at that age. Of course, if she asks sooner, I'll be honest. My guess is that she's already, at seven, beginning to sense something but can't name it, mainly because children tend not to think of their parents as sexual beings. They're just "parents."

Until I do tell her, I have to be careful in front of her not to show too much affection for Donna, to watch what I say, to pretend we're just friends. Sort of like being in public. That creates some conflict because there are certain nights when I'd like to sleep with Donna, but I'd like to have the girls sleep over too. So sometimes I choose one and sometimes the other. I don't like that compromise, but it's something I'll have to do, at least until I come out to Lisa.

At this point, I'm not sure that I'll be with Donna in another year or two, but I have a feeling that I will. I'm not sure that we'll ever live together or that she and Julie and Lisa will grow a lot closer. But we all get along fine. We enjoy going places together. She seems to like them; they seem to like her. And that's just fine for now. I don't expect them to call her "Aunt Donna" and I don't expect her to love them as if they were her own. What's more, I don't think my children need to go through another of my breakups. So for now, I'm just taking things as they come. And I don't see any problems there. I don't see any real conflict between my relationship with Donna and my relationship with Julie and Lisa.

Most of the Problems that really do exist in my life right now have nothing at all to do with my being gay. Most of my problems have to do with money, with career decisions, and all the usual, manageable problems that parents always face: babysitters, chicken pox, bee stings, and so on.

Even though I don't live with my children, I do live nearby and see them four or five times a week. I cook for them, clean up after them, tend their wounds, and press their clothes. I take them for music lessons, doctor visits, and haircuts. We have many lengthy talks about teachers, crushes, jealousy, music, art, schoolwork, clothes, hair, puberty, nutrition, right and wrong, God and religion, and life

90

in general. We shop together, cook together, and go camping together. We dance, play, laugh, argue, make up, and hold each other during thunderstorms. I really, honestly believe that I am the best mother they could have. (Fortunately, their father agrees.) And yet, there are some people who would like me to feel guilty.

My ex-mother-in-law never liked me anyway, never thought a woman should have a mind of her own. So I don't let her worry me any more.

And of course there's my father. I'm sure he'd like to see me meet some nice guy. But that's just because he cares about me and knows that it is easier to be "normal." He's never admitted it to me, but his own sister was a lesbian. I discovered that long ago (after she died, unfortunately). He always seemed to pity her. So there is an element of shame, I suppose, of harm to the family name. But the issue of my lesbianism is small in light of the many troubles my father has faced. And he does have my sympathy; after all, his son may die of AIDS. As I said, it tends to put things in perspective.

Then there is my friend Sara. She's married, the mother of two, a good mother, socially active, involved in the PTA and her church. When I told her I was moving away from the house, away from Matt and the girls, she said, "Well, I could never give up my house and my children." It hurt me to think that she believed I was giving up my children and it angered me that she would pass judgment. She lives a very "respectable" life; but what nobody else knows is that Sara and I had a brief affair about three years ago, that she still tells me she loves me, that she still asks me to have sex with her, that she really prefers

91

women, and that underneath all that normal, suburban-mom, good-wife facade is a raging lesbian. I love Sara anyway. She made her choice. I made mine.

I'm sure there are othe people who think I'm crazy and people who disrespect me. But I'd wager that for every one of them, there are at least a few who think I'm okay. So I don't worry too much any more about what people think. I refuse to feel guilty about my sexual preference. It's my business and no one else's. And I also refuse to buy into the idea that children need their mothers more than their fathers. Matt is quite capable of caring for the girls, and financially he is better able to provide a home for them. And if my children are happy with the way they're being brought up, then I won't let other people tell me they're not.

The people who worry me most are the children who go to school with my children. Because Julie and Lisa are, naturally, not that strong yet, they can be hurt much more than I by a few nasty words. And because adults tend to talk behind one's back and not to one's face, I don't have to hear from my peers the kind of remarks my kids have to hear from theirs.

* * * * *

Julie and I had another of those afternoons to ourselves recently, and she told me that it bothers her when the kids at school make fun of gays.

"It just makes me so mad that I feel like sticking up for gays," she said. "But if I did they'd think I was gay and make fun of me. So I have to keep quiet about it."

92

"Don't you think other kids at school have family secret s too?" I asked.

"Yeah, but they don't have to hear stuff like that all the time. About their own mothers. And keep quiet about it. They make me so mad!"

"I guess it would be a lot easier for you if I were straight, wouldn't it?"

"Yeah. Sometimes I just wish you were normal. I don't like being different than other kids."

"Are you different?"

"Not really. But I feel different."

"I'm sorry," was all I could say to her at first. Then we talked about how other kids are different in other ways, some from interracial marriages, some handicapped, some poor, some always getting into trouble. And we talked about how other kids have parents who live apart too. I think the talk was somewhat useful and cathartic and comforting to both of us. But we still felt the same sort of frustration in the end.

So here is my biggest Problem: I want to be a good mother. That means being honest with my children. It means instilling in them my own values and letting them be who they will be. It also means, while they are young, trying to shield them as much as possible from psychological harm.

I can't change the way most people are. But I *can* do some things: I can talk with my children. I can let Julie see that my gay friends are okay. I can, when the time comes, come out to Lisa. I can try to raise the consciousness of some adults around me and hope they teach their children well. I can encourage my children's schools to offer sex education that deals with homophobia. I can hope that my children will be strong and proud and happy. I can hope that they'll grow up still believing what Julie said to me that day last summer: "The most important thing is that you love somebody."

I won't change the world overnight. And I won't deny that it's going to be tough. But I won't ever again feel that I have to choose between being a parent and being gay.

MS. ____ IS A LESBIAN
Susan Llork

I had been married for nine years, all the while knowing something was missing. I loved my five-year-old son and thought that my feelings for his father were love . . . until I met Donna. I fell madly, passionately in love with her. Suddenly, my previous attractions to women over the years made sense. It just took the right person to reveal my unrealized Lesbianism. What I had thought was love for my husband paled into a ridiculous charade by comparison. Within a year the divorce was final and Donna and I were living together.

When my son Erich was about eleven years old,

he picked up a new favorite word. Everybody was a "fag." At first I just told him not to use the word, but finally I confronted him. "Do you know what a 'fag' is?"

"Yeah — a queer, a gay guy."

I began defending gays, reasoning with him that gays don't bother anybody, that it's not proper to taunt or make fun, etc. etc. Finally one day he asked why I should care so much about gays. I said very simply, "Because I am gay."

He looked at me kind of funny and said, "Mom, girls can't be gay."

"But I just told you I am — would I make up something like that?"

He thought it over for a minute, realized I wasn't kidding, and said very seriously, "Does Donna know?"

I couldn't help but smile at the naivete of his question, but he was so serious that I had to explain the situation to him.

We didn't talk a lot about it after that. I would bring up things now and then just to let him understand that being a lesbian is a very important part of who I am.

Erich and Donna have a very special relationship. Donna had been afraid that when I told him about us, he might turn on her as the one who broke up our family. But to this day he has never once said anything even remotely indicating he felt that way. Their special love and friendship has only grown deeper.

* * * * *

But it has not always been easy for Erich. A good friend of mine (and sister Lesbian) is a swimming teacher at the high school Erich began attending in fall 1987. Although she is not out at school, it is more or less common knowledge among the kids that "Ms. ____ is a Lesbian."

One day Erich was talking to a group of his friends when one remarked that he was in Ms. ____'s swimming class. Erich, surely without judging the ramifications of his impending statement, innocently replied, "Oh, she's a real good friend of my Mom's. I've been out to her house lots of times."

Apparently, these kids had heard the rumor. "Oh yeah? How does your Mom know *her*? She's a lezzie."

I asked Erich how he answered that one. "Well, at first I started to tell them they were crazy, that I'd known her a long time, but then I realized — you know, she *is* one of your best friends, so I figured she must be — you know. I just told the guys that you got to know her when she was the girls' basketball and softball coach and you were officiating" — which *is* how I originally got to know my friend.

I asked, "They didn't question you any further?" thinking maybe the kids realized they were on to something.

But he replied, "No, they really didn't think anything of it."

I pondered his dilemma. "Sounds like maybe sometimes you have to make things up or change them around a little to hide what you don't want your friends to find out."

"Well," he said, "it doesn't really come up. I

mean, I don't pay attention to other kids' parents, so I don't think they pay attention to what my parents do. Besides, lots of my friends' parents are divorced, so I'm really not that different."

I asked him how he describes Donna and me to his friends.

"I just say 'my Mom and her friend.' All women have other women friends. That doesn't look like anything."

"What do you think might happen if your friends found out about me?"

"Well, how would they?" His reply was defensive.

"You know I'm not ashamed of being a Lesbian," I said. "What if I was on a TV talk show or if they took a picture of me at the Pride Parade and it got in the paper?"

"If everybody at school found out," he answered, "it would ruin my life. Kids are stupid — they'd get on me. They wouldn't understand. Maybe if it didn't happen until I was in college — college kids aren't as dumb, are they?"

"I hope not," was all I could think of. "Are you ashamed of me?"

"No. But I still wouldn't want everybody to find out."

"But you told Brian," I countered.

"That's different. Brian's my friend. He'd never tell." And he's convinced.

I asked him if he every felt funny bringing any of his friends over. He looked almost hurt and said, "Of course not. I've brought lots of my friends here."

This is very true. I do wonder how he'll feel about bringing that first special girl over. But, knowing how accepting he is, I don't think it will be a problem for him. At fourteen, Erich seems very comfortable with my Lesbianism. When Donna and I went to Washington in October 1987 to participate in the March, he was glued to the TV trying to get a glimpse of us on the CNN hourly reports. He knows we participated in the Wedding and likes to kid around by calling Donna his "mean old stepmom." And he does share "our secret" with his best friend.

All this leads me to believe that I was right to come out to Erich as soon as I felt he was capable of understanding the situation. I wanted him to hear it from me; I wanted him to know while he was young enough not to have been subjected to the vicious hate, innuendo, and stereotyping in our homophobic society. Knowing his mother is a Lesbian, he would know that homosexuality is not the horrible thing it's often made out to be.

I also think my coming out to Erich will help him be open and honest with me about important things in *his* life. I can't expect honesty from him if he gets lies from me. He knows that I am out to my family and sees their acceptance. He does not see rejection of me by people who know. I always tell him, "Everybody who is important to me knows." Still, there have been those times when he has felt the need to make excuses for me to his friends. I understand that and have told him that sometimes it's necessary for me, too, to make up excuses for myself; for instance, I am not out at work.

I try to point out instances of discrimination against gays and women, so that he will recognize injustice when he sees it. I am gratified to see indignation in his reaction. I feel I am raising a son who will be neither sexist nor homophobic. In fact,

Erich has seemed to adjust to the situation so well that sometimes when I question him about others' reactions, he is surprised that I bring it up. I hope he doesn't take too much for granted, since there is still so much hate and ignorance out there.

THE STORY
THAT NEVER ENDS
Jacqueline Matthews

My name is Jacque, age 31. I've been divorced since 1984. I'm a mulatto. My parents divorced when I was three. My brother and I were raised in the South by my father's mother until I was ten, when we moved to New Jersey after my father got out of the Air Force. I also lived with my mother from time to time. At age 17 I got married.

Both my father and my ex-husband are black. My mother and present lover are white. Hmm — could get into some heavy analysis there.

My mother came out to me six years ago by inviting me to Joy MCC with her and her "roommate," but I already kind of knew.

When I came out two and a half years ago, at age 28, I had been divorced and had sole custody of my three daughters, then ages three, six, and nine, for about one year. I never gave much thought to how I would explain things (come out) to them. I was much more concerned with catching up on information about the new life-style I was beginning, experiences I had only dreamed about during my nine years of marriage.

Like many, the first contact with my new world was the bars. As a result of the time spent there, I found it difficult to give proper attention to the girls and sent Lici and Bernie, the two older children, to stay with my sister-in-law for awhile. Sabrina stayed with me. A few months later I met my present lover Debbie.

Perhaps I am fortunate or maybe it's normal, but Sabrina had no problem with Debbie living with us, taking care of her while I was at work, and going places together. I had separated from my husband when Sabrina was only a few weeks old, so she had no other living experience to relate her present one to. When she did ask about who and where her father was, I simply explained that we didn't live together because we couldn't get along.

At one time she called Debbie Poppi. I don't remember how or why she started doing that — probably because of a discussion about her having two moms instead of a mom and dad. I vaguely remember Sabrina asking if she could call Debbie daddy. I was trying to think of some other endearing term and chose Poppi, not knowing that it meant daddy in Spanish. After I found out the meaning, we asked her to use it only at home. Sabrina of course got a kick out of using the name in public just to see what kind of reaction she would get out of us. It certainly worked well when she wanted to get our attention. Mostly we gave her a "you know better" look and did our best not to smile.

My other daughters came to live with us about a year later. We were quite anxious over what their reactions to our relationship might be. At first we refrained from any open show of affection, but after a few weeks we gradually fell back into our normal behaviors. Mostly this consisted of hugging, holding hands, and lying together on the sofa when we watched TV.

We both belong to a 12-step program, and the girls would often attend the meetings with us. After a meeting everyone gives each other hugs. This is why, I guess, our hugging at home didn't seem odd to them. There were a few times, though, that I noticed Bernie smiling when she would see us holding hands or when she walked into the room and we were standing holding each other and talking.

We tried to live with the belief that, if we handled situations and questions in a relaxed and open manner, the children would respond in a similar manner. The first real test of this theory came one summer afternoon when the girls came in unexpectedly from playing. First, let me say that as a young girl I was allowed to go out and play without a shirt on until about kindergarten. When I found that Debbie still did this around the house, well, early that afternoon it was close to panic time. Not for them, mind you, but for me. When we heard them come in the back door we just looked at one another in a state of shock and nervous laughter. We sat back, played it cool, glued our eyes to the TV, and decided not to run for a shirt. This of course was not new to Sabrina. Bernie and Lici, however, were wearing shy puzzled smiles which I interpreted to mean "Is this something we shouldn't be seeing?" Bernadette, the oldest, asked why Deb wasn't wearing a shirt. We had agreed early on that since I had the most experience with children, was their mom, and Debbie felt awkward with kids period (as she never had planned on having any or being with a woman who had any), I would be the one to explain things, whenever possible. So I took the plunge and told them that it was just a comfortable thing for her to do, comparing it to men taking off their shirts to play ball or just when sitting around. "Why should it be any different for women? Right?" seemed to suffice.

We never did have any of the BIG reactions from them we feared. We did instruct them before we began attending gay/Lesbian functions that the preferred term for homosexual men was gay and not faggot, just to be safe and prevent any embarrassment for us.

Around Bernie's eleventh birthday we started reading *What's Happening to My Body?* a book for talking with children about the facts of life. When we read the chapter on homosexuality there were no questions, no giggles, everything went smoothly.

Then, a few months later, Debbie, Bernie and I were sitting together watching a program about gay and Lesbian parents. I made a comment about what I would do if in a situation like the one being discussed. Bernie looked at me and asked, "You're gay, mom?" Deb just looked at me, grinned, and shrugged her shoulders. I think I concealed my shock pretty well. I smiled too (mostly nerves) and said in my calmest grown-up voice, "Yes, you knew that." Her reply was "Unh unh, I didn't know. Really?" "Yes, really." "Debbie too?" We both laughed and Debbie answered, "Yes."

All this time we had just assumed . . . What with all the literature around the house — newsletters, gay parenting articles, various fiction books by Lee Lynch, Jane Rule and such. Why, they even found our stash of *Penthouse* and *Playboy*! The Gay Pride Picnic, Lambda pancake breakfasts and fundraisers. Well . . . that's what we got for assuming.

Shortly afterwards, Bernadette told us that as a result of an argument, a friend of hers had told some of the other kids at school that I was gay. It all passed in two or three days, but we warned her to be more careful about who she confided in and, most important, that it was no one's business who I slept with and that family matters should not be discussed outside of home. We warned Bernie that some children (or their parents) might have strong feelings about homosexuals and might not want to be friends with her. She only lost that one gossiping friend, and the only other mention of the subject at school was when a boy told her that since I was gay, she was too. Bernie told me that she told him that wasn't so. I reassured her that my being a Lesbian most certainly did not mean she was too.

The rest of the school year went well. Bernie even asked me to come to her track meets when her coach asked for parents to help out with transportation and as timers. I was hesitant at first because I anticipated stares and whispers. To my relief, I was well received by her friends; and most of all, it felt FANTASTIC that my daughter was proud to have me there.

My middle daughter, Delicia, is pretty quiet, but it is amazing to me how close she is with Debbie. She really tends to open up and confide in her more easily than with me. We often refer to her as Debbie's child. Once Lici asked me if Deb was a man.

"You know she's not a man, not with breasts like that."

"But she looks like a man."

"Well, who says that a man or woman has to look a certain way? I've seen lots of women that look like Debbie."

"But she doesn't wear make-up."

"Not all women wear make-up."

"Oh."

And that was that.

* * * * *

The next time the gay topic came up was two months later. The girls were sitting at the dinner table; I was in the living room. From the table I hear "Mom?" It's Lici (eight years old).

"Yes?"

"Are you gay?"

I swallow hard. Here we go again. I get up and go to the dining room. "Yes, I am."

Sabrina to Lici, "I told you so."

Lici smiles shyly. I ask both of them if they know what gay means.

Lici says, "It's when you like someone."

Bina adds, "Like a girlfriend."

"Yes . . . but it's a little more. It's when two women like each other or two men like each other. Mostly men are called gay and women are Lesbians."

"Oh," they reply. And once again, that was that.

I try to keep the answers and explanations simple and honest. As they get older I'm sure the questions will get more detailed, deeper. It seems that coming out is going to be a gradual and continuing process.

LESBIAN COOTIES
Judy Helfand

At first I thought an article about coming out to my children would be a description of a one-time thing. An announcement. Now I see that coming out is an on-going process, an integral part of the relationship I want to have with them. The first emotionally honest relationship I ever had was with Luke, my older child. He was the first person I felt I could be completely myself with, unselfconscious. I really credit that relationship with starting me on the path that brought me to recognizing my lesbianism, to beginning an exciting journey of personal discovery. It's important to me to maintain an emotionally honest relationship with my children. They provide me with proof that it is possible to just relax and be me without feeling judged.

Luke was six and my daughter Clio was two when I realized I was a lesbian and left my husband. Initially they didn't know what a lesbian was, so my telling them I was a lesbian didn't mean much. Since then I have made a point of talking about what it means to be a lesbian and how it affects them. They have been encouraged to express their feelings and relate incidents in their daily life that arise because of having a lesbian mom. Being honest with the children, making every effort to explain things clearly, has made me deal with some difficult issues. Children see right through sloppy thinking.

Coming out has been an on-going process of talk and observation. I love the openness we've created around the topic, the way we joke with each other about their possible future boyfriends or girlfriends, the way we can go to gay events and be comfortable together. I think they are growing up with a full acceptance of homosexuality, seeing it as no more or less than heterosexuality. Of course, they are aware of the oppression and bigotry, especially since they have felt it themselves. I try to be open about the times when I am afraid to be visible as a lesbian, or when I become the target of homophobia as I move through daily life. We have developed the concept of lesbian cooties as a way of talking about homophobia. Some people are afraid of getting lesbian cooties. We walk around the kitchen going "oooh" and acting like third graders threatening to put cooties on someone.

We live on a ranch. Life on a ranch makes explicit everyone's worst fantasies about what lesbians might do to them. The males are slaughtered, castrated, or saved for breeding. The females have more value; they lay eggs, give milk, or produce offspring. The males that are kept do little but look pretty and service the females. At a party one of our male guests made a nervous remark about the Emasculator box lying on the counter. (An emasculator is a tool used for castration.) "Just what you'd expect to find in a lesbian household," he said.

Luke is well aware of all this. Discussing ranch life has often served as a means of talking about his fear of being less valued by me because he is a boy. The value of men has been a central issue for Luke. I try to help him express his fears and have often reassured him that I love him and will always love him, as a boy or as a man. We've talked about homosexuality and heterosexuality, and about how being sexually attracted to one sex doesn't stop you from loving members of the other. Because I am a feminist lesbian, he has heard plenty about sexism, as evidenced by society as a whole and by specific individuals, so in our conversations we have to discuss more than sexual preference. Sexism is harder to talk about because it's easy to sound like you hate all men when talking about what men do. I tell him I want him to be able to go through life with his eyes open, his vision freed from the blinding lies I grew up with. He will make his own choices, but I want him to be aware of the privileges that come to him solely because he is white, male, and middle class.

Luke doesn't volunteer the information that he has a lesbian mother. He wants to blend in with his peers, to avoid the teasing he experienced to a small degree in elementary school. Keeping his mouth closed about having a lesbian mom has led to some amusing incidents, though. His first girlfriend was going away for the summer and he wanted to see her before she left. The only day available was the day of the Gay Freedom Day Parade. We suggested he invite her to the parade with us. Although not crazy about the idea, he thought he'd try to work something out — meet her afterward, perhaps. Several phone calls later, it turned out she was working that day helping her lesbian mother sell jewelry at the parade! As a woman who has felt different from my peers all my life, a perpetual outsider, I understand Luke's desire to fit in, to keep his differences to himself. I know it is not shame which motivates him.

Clio has never felt threatened by my lesbianism, as has Luke. In fact initially, at age two, she had little understanding of what it meant for me to be a lesbian, except that I was no longer living with her father. Later she equated "lesbian" with "strong woman" and was sure that she was a lesbian too. Today, at age nine, she knows sexual feelings are part of the picture. At times she has equated being a lesbian with disliking men, sometimes trying to please me by finding fault with men or boys. As with Luke, I try to make it clear that I judge each person by their own merit. When some of my women friends betrayed me and hurt me deeply, she was able to see more clearly that gender doesn't completely determine behavior.

Clio's approach has been to inform the world that her mother is a lesbian. For example, early in the year at a new school she announced proudly in an essay on world peace, "My mother is a lesbian." She challenges verbally or physically anyone who tries to tease her or make derogatory remarks about lesbians. She's more than willing to clarify any misconceptions friends may have about homosexuals. But Clio did lose one close friend because of my lesbianism. This girl, seen by both me and my lover as a possible lesbian herself, became increasingly frightened of her own sexual feelings when she was visiting with Clio. She eventually decided she was unable to see Clio in our home, but still wanted Clio to play at her home. Clio was unwilling to continue the friendship without full acceptance and stopped seeing her. It was extremely painful for her to experience this homophobia. She lost a good friend, but she was able to see it as her friend's problem and not something about her that caused the break. As a radical who has always wanted to be seen as I truly am and to say what I really think, I understand Clio's insistence on being known as the daughter of a lesbian. I admire her fighting spirit.

In addition to our individual coming-out processes, we have also had to come out as a family. Raised in the fifties, I carry with me the Dick-and-Jane formula for happy families. I know that this formula doesn't work to benefit all family members; I know that I don't want a family like that; but at the same time I realize that many people still judge families according to how they measure up to the Dick-and-Jane standard.

I judge a family by how well everyone in it is able to be their own person. It's important to discover your own talents and individual desires, to explore the world in your own way, and to feel loved by other family members simply for being who you are. Socialization is a process whereby children are often forced into a standard mold or made to feel bad because they don't fit. I don't want my children to be socialized in this way. Often I feel like I'm battling the schools, the movies, their friends, the whole world, in my efforts to let my children develop to their full potential and feel good about who they are. Lesbianism is only one part of it.

I try to keep a running dialogue going on how we are doing as a family. This means discussing problems that arise between various members. Within a family parents have more power than children. As a parent I have more responsibility for taking care of the children than they have for taking care of me (although we may have equal commitments emotionally), and I often make decisions that affect them. But I don't believe that parents have to provide a united front to the children or that parents are always right. Because of this belief, I feel that everything that goes on within the family can be discussed. On occasion the children come to me complaining about my partner, their step-mother (their term to describe her relationship to them). We talk about the problem and try to understand how her own experiences as a child may influence how she treats them. We talk about how they themselves contributed to the problem. We try to acknowledge the emotions underlying the actions so as to get to the root of the problem. I don't feel that I have to back up my partner if I don't agree with what she did, but I won't accept a blanket condemnation of her either.

I try to be open to hearing from my children about the ways I act that they don't like. A couple of years ago I had to grapple with a major problem. The

113

children had been staying with me weekdays, attending the local school, and spending weekends with their father. When Luke was in the sixth grade he wanted to reverse things and go to junior high where his father lived. Since we didn't want to separate Luke and Clio, this would have meant Clio would have to change schools too. But Clio was in a special program I didn't want to pull her out of for at least one more year, so I wanted Luke to wait one year. The whole thing turned into a battle and eventually a court mediator decided that the children should stay with me for the coming year. But Luke and Clio didn't like the decision. They felt I was being unfair and continued to tell me so. I refused to really listen to them until the day before school started. When I saw how miserable they were, especially Luke, I knew I couldn't hold them. I was able to talk about how afraid I was of losing them, how painful it was for me not to have them on a daily basis, and how scared I was of feeling a huge emptiness without them there every weekday morning. I also acknowledged my mistake in trying to force them to do what they didn't want to do. In talking about my own feelings and acknowledging my mistakes, I hope to be seen as the complex person I am, not simply as Mother, that simple two-dimensional cut-out from Dick and Jane.

We talk about other families, too. Incest, wife-beating, child abuse, and alcoholism have long been considered improper subjects for polite conversation, but my children, my lover and I discuss these topics both in general and as they occur in families we know. We talk about their friends' lives and how children are treated in society at large.

Having a lesbian mother becomes one facet of the complex structure that is their family.

I like our family. Although we're all fairly independent people, we usually enjoy the familyness of doing things together. At the movies, out to dinner, camping, or wherever we go we're always on the lookout for other gay families. We often find them. We certainly don't feel bad about who we are even when we don't. I like to think of our family as a good example in the world. For example, when we're camping the children make friends and bring them to our campsite. They can sit around and share in what we're doing, having a good time with lesbians and thereby counteracting some of the homophobic training they have probably already received. If, as once happened, someone passes by talking about "those poor kids" having to be with "those kind of people," we don't pretend it didn't happen but laugh about how wrong they are. As a mother who insists on being who I am with my children, I do my best to keep this continuing coming-out process alive. It's exciting to grow with children. Whatever the future brings, it's unlikely to be boring.

OUR FAMILY
Delia Cunningham

There are plenty of reasons why people choose to have children. Usually, however, they don't choose. They simply let it happen and do nothing to change their fate once conception has occurred. This is even the case for some lesbians who back into parenting by slipping into heterosexuality just long enough to get caught. The difference, of course, is the intent.

For my partner of 11 years and me, motherhood was definitely by choice. When we met, we were both professionals — she at athletics and I at writing. She was a divorcee. I had been engaged to a man before falling madly in love with a college sorority sister, a serious relationship that lasted four years.

When I met my lover and parenting partner, she was a stepmother who had raised one boy to near puberty. I knew I wanted to be and was meant to be — one day — a mother.

The first time I met her son was several months later. She was not able to get custody of the boy since he was biologically the father's, despite the fact the child's biological mother had not seen or contacted him since he was removed from her as an abused 5-year-old. Unfortunately, my lover had also been subjected to abuse from her ex-husband and traded all financial and real assets for the "privilege" of seeing their son — at the father's total discretion. Visits, usually allowed when the boy needed new clothes, braces or some other financial attention, were rare but treasured.

Larry was a gentle boy, more like his stepmother than his biological parents. Still, he was Sheryl's son only by her former marriage. She had no control. We had to be careful.

When Larry came to visit us for more than a few hours, we were careful to avoid showing too much affection. With no legal rights and a suspicious father (who wanted *both* of us to have sex with him despite his new, young wife), we did not want to put our boy in a situation where he had to lie. If he saw nothing, he could say he saw nothing.

At the same time, it wasn't long before Larry knew his mother and I were more than friends. We slept (nothing more) in the same room together during his visits, always leaving the door open. He was welcome to join us in the mornings, and some evenings he would lie between us watching television from bed. We felt warm and cozy, a special kind of family.

Finally, the time came when Larry was himself the victim of his father's abuse. He ran away from there to our home. Larry was then 11. He said he wanted to change his name to Sheryl's. He wanted to live with us. We gave him shelter but always had to face the reality of law. Sheryl was only his stepmother, and that relationship was no longer legitimate.

We knew if we went to court, Larry's father would accuse us of lesbianism. It was time to come out to Larry, especially if we were going to fight the system for him. On a weekend away we began to explain that the two of us loved each other very much, and we both loved him. We told him the love we shared was very normal and very special, although at that time we didn't give it a name. We did explain that we were a couple just like a man and a woman could be a couple, and that many people, including his father, would use that against us.

So he could tell the judge we did not sleep together, we put twin beds in our room. It felt a bit awkward to make that move, but we did not know what strength our young man had in him. We did know how brutal his father could be.

The coming out went well. It was no news to Larry, for ours was perhaps the most stable relationship he had ever experienced. He simply accepted what we said without surprise or significant comment.

The custody battle failed. The state system beat

us, demanding that Larry be returned to his father, where he was forced to turn on us to defend his own existence in the battlefield of his father's home. We never got to court. Larry was just not strong enough. Sheryl was ordered never to see her son again so long as he was a minor.

The next two years were difficult for us. We separated temporarily. We met others, we cried and we reunited. We grew immensely. And during that time I began to plan for a not-too-distant day when I would have my own children, with or without a partner. It was a decision I knew intuitively was right for me.

Sheryl and I healed, loved and finally made peace together. As we became close again, we knew even more surely that we were meant to parent together. We dreamed of the possibility of having children together and began to explore the ways that might happen.

The year was 1980. The options were limited. Our inquiries revealed there was no sperm bank or doctor in the state (that we could locate) who would inseminate an unmarried woman. An attorney told us there was no legal or tactical way either or both of us could adopt even a special needs child and be protected from losing the child should anyone question our lifestyle. We had already lost one child. We did not intend to lose another.

Finally, we decided one of us had to birth a child if we wanted to be parents. Physical circumstances and financial considerations such as insurance made the decision for us that I should be the one to become pregnant. We began to make inquiries among the women we knew of how the turkey baster method worked and what we should do. We began to evaluate the available men to select as donors, a decision based on the unavailability of anonymous sperm as well as on our desire that our children at least be able to know their father's name.

The first man we approached did not take us seriously at the time. Later, he wished he had, but by then it was too late.

The second man saw a possibility for himself to be a "surrogate father" for us as a couple, giving us the child we longed for. After discussing it with his lover of several years and between the four of us, he agreed.

With an enormous amount of luck, a haphazard bit of instruction in technique and timing, and plenty of love, we achieved pregnancy through homemade artificial insemination. It was a one-shot success, proving to our inner selves that Aaron, whom I birthed that fall, was meant to be a part of our family. This beautiful, perfectly formed little boy began the most wonderful adventure of our lives.

As an only child, I was determined to keep my own offspring from that same fate. Believing siblings are one of the most valuable gifts a parent can give a child, my lover and I began to expand our family.

Things were changing on the adoption scene. Of course, lesbians and gays could not openly adopt, but a friend in a neighboring community told us about other women who were closeted lesbians receiving older children from a state agency. It was an opportunity for my lover to bring a child into our family — one with her name, yet a sibling for our son.

Still, the process was not easy. We temporarily

accepted a troubled 6-year-old into our home, but she became so violent we feared for our toddler's safety. The situation could not work. We had to give up.

My lover tried to get pregnant in spite of the physical barriers we knew existed. She was not succeeding, and our son was getting older. We wanted him to have a sibling to share his childhood with, and this time we hoped for a girl.

With advice from a feminist midwife on how to influence the gender of a fetus, I began the Preconception Gender Diet. I could stay on it for six months without danger, but after three months we reached a point where my lover still had not become pregnant and felt she needed to skip a month in trying. Without intellectually knowing why, I turned to her one evening and told her it was time for me to try. Again, I had not checked my ovulation or any of the other things one is supposed to do when trying to get pregnant. I just knew the time was right.

Our donor arrived the next evening and we repeated the process using the same implements as always. That August our daughter was born, right on schedule. We were thrilled.

The surprise came, however, five weeks later. My lover was home alone, since I had gone to a La Leche League meeting (a support group for nursing mothers). Our friend from the state agency called. There was a mixed race baby about to be surrendered for adoption. She could have her if she agreed right then. There was no time for decision making, no time for discussion. If she delayed, the child would be sent to foster care.

Mothering was not my desire alone. We had considered having more children, possibly being pregnant together. We had discussed a biracial adoption. My lover saw her chance to be a mother to a child who would carry her name and be considered hers by "straight" society. Again, the time was right. Our second daughter had arrived.

Our family is unlike the others on our block, and unlike the others in our community. There are no legally recognized fathers to challenge our custody of these three loving children. Other than for the fact we are lesbian mothers, we go overboard to lead a legal, moral lifestyle in the eyes of the society around us. Oh, we are politically active as much as possible, taking our children and showing them how and why we must work for change in the world. We do not pretend we are just like other families; we know we are different. That is a part of our coming out.

At one month old our son was part of a pro-choice march and a pro-ERA demonstration. He has attended women's music festivals and full moon circles. Once he even went to a gay restaurant/bar with both of us, his daddy and his papa, who have become even better friends with us since our son's birth.

Our girls, now 2-year-olds, have had less opportunity to experience our daily coming out. We've taken them to political demonstrations and marches, of course. They've been to gay picnics and to lesbian and/or gay parent gatherings when we attempted to have some. They've been to NOW meetings and conferences, mainly because that is the one feminist group that ever offers child care.

As the mothers of three young children, there are few places for our family to go within the gay and lesbian community. The MCC Church welcomes gays but offers nothing for our children. Instead, we attend the Unitarian Universalist Church, where we even dared to have our family photo (yes, all five of us) taken for the church yearbook. And when there is a gay and/or lesbian event held in a public place such as a state park, we go with our children knowing they cannot be turned away. So far they have always been accepted.

We have not gone to women's events where child care is segregated by gender, refusing to perpetuate patriarchal dichotomy into another generation. Our son, like our daughters, will have a great responsibility as an adult with a raised consciousness. They may or may not choose to become politically active, but they will inevitably live a lifestyle that comes from a personal understanding of oppression as well as of mutual loving support. And whatever family style they select will be chosen with a knowledge of what family truly means.

Our son is now 6, which places him in kindergarten in our state. He hears the words lesbian and gay used in his home with comfort, and he sees our gay and lesbian friends sharing appropriate affection. We see this as natural and vital to our children's experience. If we do not accept them into our community, our lifestyle, how can we expect them to feel we are a part of their future? There must be a place for their generation, for lesbian-feminist raised children whose upbringing avoided sexual stereotypes and assigned roles.

Aaron knows his family is not like that of other children, but then again he knows we are not so different. He and his sisters have two parents, both of whom are women. He knows his mommy and his nana (his name for my lover) love each other, sleep together and share finances and responsibilities. He knows he has two special friends — his daddy and his papa — who love him and love each other and live together. When he spends the night at their house, he sleeps between them in their big, cozy water bed. He knows he is loved.

Our coming out to our children is continual. We are their parents. It would be ever so wrong to hide our love for each other. It is from our sincerity and truth, from our workings of our relationship with each other and with them that they will build their self-esteem and their vision of their futures. How could we not be true to ourselves and honest with them?

Aaron was in preschool when he first asked about his nana and me. He wanted to know if we were married, and if his daddy and papa were married. I said we were, in a way. I told him we loved each other, and that his nana and I had shared a special ceremony like people do when they get married. But I also told him there is a thing called law, and that legally I was not married to his nana or to anyone.

In our discussion of this thing called marriage, we also talked about the choices a person makes in life. We have a single woman friend who chose to have her child without a partner. We have lesbian and gay friends who are couples but have no children. We even discussed a few straight friends.

It took several excursions into that conversation on a number of different occasions before he began to understand. Eventually he wanted to know about sex,

124

about how babies were made and about how he was made (which was definitely different). Using simple language and picture books (such as there are), he learned the basics appropriate for his age.

Now he is in kindergarten. When it was his special week, he selected photos of his family to take to school and post on the bulletin board. There were photos of Mommy and Nana, photos of his sisters, photos of his daddy and papa, and a photo of his grandparents. When we discussed this with his teachers later, she told us with surprise that she didn't believe he realized his family was different from any other.

Suddenly, she saw it was. But what she recognized was two parents who cared enough about their child to inquire in depth about what happened in his school days and about his overall well being. She was professional. She didn't miss a beat.

We have made some concessions, of a sort. Since we live in my home town, when the first two children were born we had a blessing (similar to a christening) for each of them. The ceremonies were performed by a woman minister who did not use patriarchal religious terms. They were highly spiritual and personal events. In each ceremony Sheryl was acknowledged as the child's godparent, giving my biological family a clear indication of the person with whom these little ones would live should anything happen, and giving Sheryl an acknowledged, legitimate role in their upbringing.

When Sheryl had to be approved for adoption, we made sure she had her own bedroom in the house (although it was never used). I avoided contact with the social workers and, while she never had to deny her lesbianism, she sidestepped the issue to avoid confrontation.

This is not an open-minded, free world. This is not even California. We live in the South, although in a tourist-oriented arts community. My birth name does not appear on this essay, and the names within have been changed to protect the children — just in case. Still, we are not so far in the closet that our family cannot see the light.

At the same time, we have a family that is creating a future. It is my sincere desire that we may share that future in the heart of our gay and lesbian communities as lesbian mothers, with children nurtured by a culture sensitized by its past and optimistic about its future. These are the children who will, indeed, be changing the world in which we will grow old.

This can only happen if we create a place for our children in all of our lives and in our alternative communities, which too often greet little ones with question, rejection and fear. If they are not spurned by or left out of the alternative world that inspired the possibility of their birth, they may live to see, to create, and to be a part of a world that brings true equality and hope. With the support of our spiritual community, they may be the generation that sparks a future of freedom and awakening about which we can only dream.

IV
WORKING IT THROUGH:
PROBLEMS OF COMING OUT

Coming out has always been problematic for gay men and Lesbians. Coming out to ourselves requires changes in our lives, changes that may be very hard and very costly. Coming out to our parents brings with it the risk of isolation, disapproval, loss. Coming out at work carries financial risk. And coming out to our children combines these risks. In one sense our lives are complicated in exactly the same ways everyone's lives are complicated — we have relationship problems, we face the difficulties of being single parents, we experience custody battles just as straight parents do. But the Lesbian or gay parent bears additional burdens caused by homophobia.

There are the legal burdens. Given the current legal climate in most states (see section V), many parents must balance their desire to be out against a legal system which declares homosexuals unfit parents. In such a climate, to tell one's children may be to risk losing them.

The burden of ex-spouse response is often linked to the legal burden. Homophobia can create irrational behavior in a former mate who seeks justification for his or her anger through stigmatizing a gay or Lesbian parent. Children's loyalties can be divided and manipulated. All too often, knowledge of sexual orientation can be a time bomb, and we can but wait to see if it explodes.

Coming out also affects our living patterns. The relationship between a Lesbian or gay parent and her or his lover may be partly determined by the presence of children. Do we call our lovers "roommates"? Do we deny ourselves love in order to protect our children? Do we live with our lover or with our children?

Finally — perhaps most to be feared — are the burdens generated by the homophobic conditioning all children receive in American culture. If we tell, we risk exposing our children to ridicule, ostracism, or stigma. A child rejected by peers may turn anger onto parents. In an attempt to proclaim "normality," children may alienate themselves from Lesbian and gay parents. While this happens much less frequently than we might expect (or fear), it remains a risk which we cannot overlook.

The stories in this section show some of the difficulties of coming out to our children. They also suggest some ways parents contemplating coming out to their children might approach the issue.

FINDING WAYS
TO COMMUNICATE
Sharon Joyce

March 4, 1988

There was never a question of *not* coming out to my boys. I never considered keeping the truth from them — the only question was how and when, not if. So much joy to share — how could they ever know me if they did not know who I loved? If I failed to share my deepest joy and my most empowering understanding of myself, didn't I make their own emotions less clear to themselves? If they did not

129

know the source of the strength that propelled me through time of stress and confusion, how could they understand my life at all? And if they did not understand my life, how could they ultimately connect with their own deepest level of emotion or with the emotions of any other person? Coming out to them seemed important right from the start, and I have never had a reason to regret my decision. The saddest words I can imagine would be "I never knew her well."

Just five years ago — not so long in time, but a millennium in terms of growth and strength. It's so clear now how ready I was for the magic of a relationship with a woman when I met Kelly. I believe I fell in love with her the day she walked into the office. Within 5 months of having seen her for the first time, I came out to myself, came out to her, and decided that no matter what she chose to do, my own marriage was over and I was going in search of the life I had turned away from so many years before.

I began keeping a journal in 1972, the year Bob and I decided to have a baby — the second year of our marriage. I got the idea from a fiction piece in *Redbook* magazine. In that story, a woman begins a journal and ultimately talks herself out of her marriage. I recall feeling smug as I read the story — divorce would never be my experience! But the journal itself sounded like a nice way to express some of the many feelings it seemed I could not comfortably share with Bob. Daily, weekly, whenever I felt like it, I wrote. Alex was born in 1973 and Corey came along in 1975 and still I wrote. Nothing great, nothing earth shattering, just the words of the ordinary life of an ordinary woman. I thought maybe some day the boys would enjoy reading what life was like for me. I still believe it, but for reasons that, in those days, I would never have understood.

November 17, 1982: A new woman began work today. I think I'm going to like her a lot. She is quite beautiful and we laugh at the same things. There is something different about her that intrigues me.

December 23, 1982: Christmas vacation starts tomorrow. Kelly and I stood at the window and looked out at the snow while she told me how glad she was to have a chance to go home and see her family. She's been looking forward to this, but I find that all I've been doing is counting the days until we get back to work and I can see her again. Certainly I've never done that before.

January 15, 1983: This woman — this strange and wonderful woman. We went out for coffee after work and talked until 5 PM. I am stunned. Stunned that I would dream of doing that when I used to rush home as if pursued by mad dogs; stunned that she makes me laugh and feel new and wonderful; stunned that in unguarded moments I find myself imagining what it would be like to make love to her. (How can I even say such a thing? What if Bob read this?) Am I going crazy? But if this is crazy, it's right for me!

January 27: 1983: I am dizzy with thoughts — dizzy and giddy and elated and terrified. Tonight I had wine and conversation with the women in our 'Book Club' — nothing exciting, I thought as I left home. Just a chance to get away for a bit and relax.

Bob and the boys are home and doing well. I deserve this time away. How could I have known it would change my life?!

Joyce mentioned it first; she just found out some woman she knows is a lesbian, wasn't that interesting? Heads nodded — yes indeed, most interesting. (What a liberal group we are.) But I was rooted to the spot. Lesbian? And in one second, a lifetime of puzzles fell into place. How could it have happened so quickly? How could it have taken so long? The minute the word was out of her mouth, I KNEW — I UNDERSTOOD — LESBIAN!!

I said nothing, just sat and sipped my wine and went crazy with joy on the inside. I think I grinned all the way home.

February 4, 1983: My first thoughts: Bob. The boys. Do they have to know? Can I keep this to myself? Can it be my secret? Can I stay married? I need to talk to a woman who understands, but I am suddenly terrified of Kelly. What if I'm wrong about her and she isn't a lesbian? Maybe she won't want to be friends any more. I wonder if there are any books for me to read?

February 20, 1983: Suddenly, Kelly drives me crazy. I can't stay away from her but when we are together I can't say what I need to say and more than once I have just sat and looked at her, praying she could read my mind. She keeps asking what's wrong, but how can I tell her? And what on earth am I going to do? I need her and I need her friendship and I need to talk to her for hours and I need so much that I have never had. Bob wonders what is wrong and the boys must surely feel neglected and I still haven't found anyone to talk to or any books to read.

March 1, 1983: I think I have taken the first step on the road to sanity. I found a book called *Lesbian Nation* by a woman named Jill Johnston. I have read and read and even keep the book in the car (under the seat) just to have it near me like a friend. I am beginning to realize that other women have felt this same desperation and that I am not crazy but only going through an incredible experience. I don't think this is something to go through alone but I don't know who to talk to!! I never eat any more. Even Kelly mentioned how thin I look. I wonder if she could ever love me?

March 5, 1983: I found a book telling kids about sex; it's upbeat and not very clinical, and it even has one sentence in it about how some people love other people of the same sex. I bought it at once and brought it home for Alex and Corey. We read it last night and they had lots of questions. It's a first step. Just the seed of the idea that it's OK to be gay. What a very long way we have to go and I haven't even begun to deal with Bob. I am terrified of him now — terrified that once he finds out (and surely in time I will tell him) he will somehow prevent me from being on my own.

Can he do that? Does he have that kind of power?

March 17, 1983: More reading — more stress — more weight lost. I feel trapped and invisible. No one knows me anymore. I have nowhere to go — no one to talk to and only a few books. I must talk to Kelly. I have a feeling she would understand even if she isn't Lesbian. I want her to meet Alex and Corey.

She would be great with kids. I need this woman in my life. I need to be close. She makes me realize that I have never been really close to anyone in my entire life.

March 22, 1983: We're off work for a day next week and I have decided to ask Kelly over for lunch. Sounds simple, doesn't it? Why does the idea just terrify me? Lately I can barely utter a coherent sentence in her presence. I can't concentrate on my work. I can't sleep and I never eat. Maybe I am going to die. Bob wonders why I am getting so thin but he doesn't ask a lot of questions. I suppose he is afraid of the answers. The boys don't seem to notice anything but I really feel as if I am neglecting them dreadfully.

March 25, 1983: I asked her to lunch!! First she said she would love to, but that she was sure she couldn't. She didn't say why, but I had the feeling it had something to do with the woman she lives with. I don't think I want to know any details about that. I'm not ready to deal with it. Anyway, later she called me at home and said she had changed her mind and would love to come for lunch. Talking to her on the phone leaves my knees weak.

April 4, 1983: She was right on time and we sat down on opposite sides of the dining room table and talked and talked. She looked lovely and sweet and innocent and I knew that she would say nothing about lifestyles unless I brought it up first. She talked a lot about the woman she has lived with, off and on, for 18 years. I was pierced with jealousy for all the years I did not know her and all the things she did without me. Irrational I'm sure, but real.

Finally I told her — blushing and terrified — I told her I loved her. She hugged me and said she thought she had been falling in love with me and we wondered what on earth we are going to do. Sitting here now, alone, I am almost worse off than before. Nothing is clear. How will I ever manage a divorce? What about the boys? My parents? Our friends? Her friends? I am overwhelmed with fear. What on earth can I ever tell Alex and Corey that will make them understand? Their world will be shattered at the ages of 8 and 10 and it will fall to me to repair it somehow, someday. How can it have come to this?

April 8, 1983: Perhaps it really isn't worth it. Perhaps just giving it all up and turning away from women is really the best choice. If I die inside maybe that's the sacrifice mothers make.

April 9, 1983: Bob is asking questions now. He found *Lesbian Nation* and immediately thought of Kelly. I'm frightened for both of us.

April 13, 1983: I have no idea what to say to Alex and Corey. I think I'll just wait. What would I tell them anyway? I have no idea how I even feel. Kelly can't help. She and her lover have their own issues to work out and I can't help her and she can't help me. We can't even talk anymore because Kelly promised her lover that she would stay away from me while they try to work things out. I think I was happier before I met her and fell in love!!

April 25, 1983: The boys had a day off school so I called in sick and the three of us went shopping and had lunch. We laughed a lot and had a wonderful time and I was struck with terror at the idea I might lose them or that they'd hate me. What can I say? I try to be casual and talk about Kelly in glowing terms but I realize it means nothing to them. What do they care about my adult friends? How can I tell them this woman will change their lives?

May 2, 1983: Spring. Kelly is going to Nashville for the summer and won't be back until August. She plans to leave when school is out. She thinks that a summer apart will help us sort out our feelings for each other. I don't think mine need sorting out, although sometimes being around her is like rubbing a raw wound. There is never any time to talk and there is so much that needs to be said. We owe ourselves some time together, but I am afraid of making Bob even more angry and she is afraid of upsetting Jill. How on earth is this ever going to work out?

May 8, 1983: Someone to talk to at last! Joyce introduced me to Sue, a Lesbian who lives right here in town!! We talked for hours. Bob won't like her any better than he likes Kelly, but I need her friendship too badly to care.

May 20, 1983: Kelly is getting ready to leave. Only five more days. Bob is threatening to cause us to lose our jobs — call the boss and all that. I live in a constant state of terror. I have no control over my life anymore, and yet I am also aware that I have caused all of this. I threw my life to the wind, and now I can't direct where it takes me. I am at the center of a whirlwind and everything familiar is being swept away. Only Alex and Corey are untouched — and in time, even that will change. I cling to them as the one bit of sanity in my world. How could I ever survive without them?

June 2, 1983: She is gone. Bob is after me every

minute we are together — threats, pleading, tears. I sense his desperation but I can't let it affect me. I have desperation of my own. My own existence seems so fragile; how can I reach out to comfort him? How can it have come to this? If it weren't for Sue I would go entirely over the edge.

June 5, 1983: I told Alex and Corey about the divorce. It was hard. Corey cried and cried and Alex looked stunned and abandoned. How can I be doing this? Where is Kelly?

June 10, 1983: Bob doesn't come home a lot of nights and the boys and I go over to Sue's and eat dinner and watch TV. Bob has told them that Sue is the cause of the divorce and they aren't sure they like her — and yet, they really can't help liking her. They came in the kitchen once and she had her arm around my shoulder. It embarrassed them but it was good. I was able to talk to them later and explain that when women care about each other, they often show it by touching.

June 15, 1983: It feels to me like the world is caving in. Most of the time I just go through the motions because it takes all my energy just to deal with *me* and my feelings. I have nothing left for anyone else. Yet today, it seemed that I *must* begin to be honest with Alex and Corey. I'm afraid Bob is dropping hints to them that I have turned into some kind of demon, and I suppose from his standpoint, that's true. So I fixed a snack and we went up to the loft and I asked them what Bob had been telling them about me. They looked at each other and waited and then Alex said, "Nothing." So I told them that love is a wonderful thing and that I loved them with all my heart and we hugged and Corey cried.

What to say about Kelly and me was a lot harder. I told them that people are capable of loving many people and that sometimes we fall in love without meaning to. They looked blank and I knew I had no idea what the idea of love meant to them. Why are there no rules for these kinds of things? Anyway, I said there are special names for people who love people of the same sex. Names that sometimes kids use on the playground as kind of an insult, but that didn't mean it was bad to love a person of the same sex. I asked them if they had heard anyone call anyone "gay" and they nodded and looked confused. I don't think they had associated "gay" with any kind of love. They just knew it was bad. So I said there were other words too, like "lesbian," and that a lesbian was a woman who loved another woman like some women loved men.

Corey asked for another cookie and Alex didn't say a word. They have no idea what to say and it's wrong for me to expect much. I can't become a woman so desperate she would look to her 8- and 10-year-old children for emotional understanding.

June 17, 1983: Alex says Bob makes nasty remarks about the women I know. That must be why both boys are acting so standoffish. They are caught in a war of words — his and mine.

June 20, 1983: Alex has acted upset lately. He cries easily and looks lost and miserable. Today I sat down with him and just started to talk. I didn't really press him to tell me how he felt, I just told him how I felt (some of it) and how difficult all this is and yet how we can survive if we stick together. I talked about Kelly too, but I am aware that until he

138

gets to know her, my good words about her won't be enough to counteract Bob's bad words.

July 1, 1983: It's too late to go back; we've come too far, too much has been said and too much has been done that can never be undone. But, if I could, just for one day, I think I would go back. Life was so simple then.

July 6, 1983: I took the boys to see my parents for a few days. It was great to get away from the stress. I'm still talking to the boys, but it's hard to be too specific. I'm afraid that they might tell someone else (or my parents) and I also want to avoid giving them the idea that Kelly is the cause of the divorce.

July 10, 1983: Bob must have found a lawyer. He came home telling me he *will* have the boys and that it would probably be better if I never saw them again. I'm shocked and the terror starts all over again. For so long now he's been saying he'll just leave this part of the country and never come back — and now this. He's urging me to leave now to see if "I really want this." I'm afraid if I do he'll claim I abandoned the family and he really will get the kids for good.

July 17, 1983: We talked briefly about my keeping one boy and him keeping the other, but I really don't want to separate them and in the end he decided that he wanted both of them anyway. He seems torn between hating me and feeling pity. His family is outraged over the Lesbian issue and they are urging him to take me to court. I have a desperate feeling that I don't have much time left with the boys.

August 5, 1983: Kelly is back. Back in the state,

anyway, but living in another town. We did manage to get away for three days — don't ask me how. I was scared to death the whole time that we would be caught, but it was worth the risk. I haven't seen her in so long.

August 26, 1983: Bob is out looking for a place to live. He'll be gone soon. He wants the boys to live with him and I am too scared to fight it out in court. Kelly and I could lose our jobs, my folks would find out, and besides, this town is *tiny* and everyone would know, and what on earth would come of that? The fight could destroy Kelly and me even before we have begun and I can't see that Alex and Corey would benefit from that. If I had known when we started out where it all was heading, would I have done it differently? Like Sue says, I want to know how it ends, but from here, it's more than just a bit uncertain.

September 12, 1983: Bob is still looking for a house. Now he says that he will let me keep the boys for this school year. Neither one of us wants to take them out of school in the middle of the year, and he doesn't know when he will find another house.

At times my heart bleeds for him. The worst of it is, he is a good man. He never ran around or drank or spent money foolishly. He came home after work and we did things as a family and we believed we were happy. He will never understand what changed me so suddenly. I told him once I was like a time bomb, just waiting to go off. There is nothing he could have done differently that would have prevented the final explosion. I think that idea makes me sad. Sometimes I wish very much that this story could have ended differently. Yet even as I wish for something easier, I know that to deny who I am, and remain married for the sake of the children or my parents or society or even for Bob, would be to deny something so basic in myself that, in the end, it would kill my deepest sense of who I am and what my life means.

September 25, 1983: Kelly is still struggling with Jill. They have many issues and a lot of love and respect for each other and a futile wish to end it without pain. I can't help or even fully understand. I respect what they have had with all my heart but I will fight for Kelly to the bitter end. (Does that sound wildly dramatic?)

October 15, 1983: Bob signed the final papers on his new house and then took Corey and Alex and me over to see it. The next door neighbors walked over to welcome "us" to the neighborhood and I felt such a deep sense of pain and loss that I had to walk away and sit in the car. I don't want to have to deal with anything else.

October 23, 1983: Kelly's birthday. I got her a card and wanted it to be so much more. Jill will take her out to dinner and I will go home alone. Self pity? I can't deny that I feel that I have given up everything — I have done all that I can possibly do, now I just have to wait until she is ready to leave.

November 6, 1983: Sue and I have tickets for the Holly Near concert. So do Kelly and Jill. Bob has the boys this weekend for the first time. I am truly alone at last. I wonder if I will see her at the concert?

November 20, 1983: Just more waiting. Sue and I have gotten into the habit of getting together on

Friday after the boys leave and drinking wine and listening to women's music and talking and talking. She is the only person I can really talk to — the only person I have the energy to deal with any more. If I didn't have Friday night to look forward to, I don't think I could survive the week.

December 1, 1983: Bob has a girl friend. They bring the boys back late on Sunday night and he is full of anger. Perhaps she gives him the courage to confront me. The other Sunday they broke the storm door when they came in and he just walked off and left me to try to fix it in the freezing cold. If he doesn't care for me at all, what about the boys? I think they have become his weapons.

December 10, 1983: The year draws to a close. Last Christmas this was just barely starting. I had no idea then what lay ahead. Life is full of tricks. I cling to the idea that after the first of the year Kelly will move out and get an apartment of her own even if she doesn't move in with me. Yet the idea of her moving in here scares me to death right now. What about Corey and Alex? How would they take it? I haven't begun to make them understand what all this means. I have a desperate feeling that they must be totally accepting before she arrives, and yet how much can they understand when they are only 9 and 11? I just don't have any guidelines for what to do or how to handle it.

December 23, 1983: I broke down and invited Bob to spend Christmas with me and the boys at my folks' house. He was sad and lonely and I couldn't stand the idea of letting him be alone. My folks are delighted and so are the kids. I wouldn't be spending the day with Kelly anyway. She and Jill are going to their parents' houses. I find I am living on the thin edge of oblivion.

January 3, 1984: Back to work. Kelly had a dreadful vacation filled with tears and fights with Jill. Being alone with the boys all week is grinding me down. I sit alone and write in my journal after they go to bed, and lately I have been filled with panic. I have an overwhelming fear that someone will come along and drag me back — deny me the right to be independent and live the life I choose. What kind of mother can I possibly be right now? Bob is no better at being a father. The boys are silent. How long can we all endure?

January 27, 1984: Bob came into the house and stole the letters Kelly had written to me. Now he calls very late at night, filled with anger. He demands that I give up the boys. He says that no judge in the world would ever let me have them. He does not even know if he will ever let me see them again. I am tempted to take them and run away. I understand kidnapping by the "non-custodial parent." I feel unclean. No one in their right mind would want to be around me if they knew the truth. I told Kelly he had stolen the letters and now we are both scared to death.

February 9, 1984: I think the divorce will come through soon. I don't think any of us can stand much more of this. I don't know yet if Kelly will really leave Jill even if I do get a divorce. I just live one day at a time and try to keep the panic at bay.

March 10, 1984: The boys and I got home about 11 PM last night after Book Club at Joyce's. We had just gotten back home when someone knocked on the door. I sent the boys downstairs and went to the door only to see Kelly standing there. I must have screamed because the kids rushed upstairs in a panic and it took us some time to calm them down again. I can barely describe how it felt to have her here. The boys wondered why she came and if she was going to stay and, of course, where she was going to sleep. "With you?" Alex looked shocked. I just said that of course she was, and tried to act as if it were an everyday event. They'll just have to get used to the idea.

March 21, 1984: The divorce was final today. I actually sat in the judge's chambers and signed a document giving Bob "Primary Physical Custody" of Alex and Corey. Have I betrayed them? Could I have fought for them and kept the rest of the puzzle pieces together at the same time? Will they believe I abandoned them (and I feel sure that is exactly what Bob will tell them)? Yet it's over and I am free at last. I have a deep confidence that Kelly and I can handle whatever comes. At least I have them every weekend and every summer. Surely that will be enough time for us to establish a new relationship based on a new reality.

Sue went with me to the court house. I felt angry and determined and sad and distant. Tonight I'm going to Kelly's to spend the weekend. Jill has gone to Nashville to look for a job.

April 15, 1984: Mr. Fieldman told Kelly today that the board decided not to renew her contract. She has been fired. We are all in a panic. She is sure it's because of us and we both feel shamed and dirty. What will we do now?

May 17, 1984: Kelly moved in today. We spent the weekend moving her things. Now it begins — the long wait is over. I have convinced her not to look for another job just yet. She is going to apply to graduate school at the city college and get a Master's degree in Social Work.

June 28, 1984: Corey confided in a friend of his that I am gay. I have dreaded this. The next day at the swimming pool three or four little boys began to tease him about me. He is hurt and feels betrayed. I am terrified that someone will believe them. I just told Alex that no one else needs to know this. I assured him that I am not ashamed of being gay, but that many people would not understand and there is no need for them to know about something that is none of their business anyway. Now he is learning about family secrets. I hope we can all survive.

October 17, 1984: The boys are both so angry when we pick them up on Friday nights that they pout or fight or cry all the way home. Kelly is so good with them. Without her I would literally fall apart. One Friday she was out of town so I picked them up alone and was going to take them out for dinner. I had looked forward to it all day, but they were so full of anger and frustration that I lost my temper and actually put Alex out of the car on the road because I couldn't take it anymore. I wasn't going to drive off, but Corey thought I was and he completely fell apart. I decided just to take them home and eat hot dogs. Maybe Bob is right. Maybe I'm not fit to be a mother.

October 23, 1984: Kelly and I talk about the boys all the time. Over and over we discuss how to deal with them and how to handle our own feelings. She helps me talk about my anger and frustration and then I seem to be able to cope with the boys in a more positive manner. They won't tell us how angry they feel. Maybe they don't even know. But they say that no one at school likes them, and Corey gets in fights. I don't know if it would be any different if they lived with us or not.

December 13, 1984: We are planning our first Christmas together. Alex and Corey are getting along better at school. We haven't had as many fights on the way home on Fridays. Maybe we're making some progress.

February 14, 1985: We spend so much time talking that sometimes I am worn out with words. Alex has a couple of friends at school that he seems to like. Corey is still running around with the tough kids in his class. He doesn't think his teacher likes him and his grades aren't as good as they should be.

April 4, 1985: The first year is almost over. I can't wait until Alex and Corey are back here to live for awhile. They keep talking about coming home. I'm glad they still think of this as home. Corey is anxious a lot. Last week Kelly went to her folks' house for the weekend and he was depressed the whole time. He craves stability. I think he is afraid she might leave for good.

May 25, 1985: I picked the boys up yesterday and brought them here. The summer seems to stretch away as far as the eye can see, filled with wonderful possibilities. We have endured a lot in the last year. Alex and Corey and I have really had to create an entirely new relationship based on a whole different idea of who a mother is and what she does. Oddly enough, I like them a lot better than I used to. I think being in a happy relationship with Kelly has taught me a lot about how to love someone — them included. The best part is, we have learned to talk and learned to listen. I find it so much easier now to hear what they have to say, even if I don't agree. I guess I no longer believe I have to control all their thoughts. (Could I ever have been so foolish as to believe it was possible?) I will never know what it cost them emotionally to give up their cherished notions of what mothers should be and accept me for what I am and have become. There has been pain in this for all of us, and perhaps we will never completely put the pain behind us. Maybe that's what life is all about anyway.

The other day I was talking to Alex about his future and what he might do. I warned him jokingly not to even *think* about getting married before he finished graduate school. He just laughed and said, "What if I'm gay?" I guess if he can kid me about it, things must be OK with him.

August, 1988: Alex is 15 now and a sophomore in high school. Corey is in the 7th grade and loves to play football. Kelly and I are still together and as much in love as we were in the beginning.

Alex and Corey seem perfectly comfortable with having a lesbian mother. It's not news they ever share with their friends that I know of, but they don't seem to feel personally burdened by the fact their family is slightly unconventional. We take a deep delight in each other and I believe that part of the reason is that our time together is so special since it is rather short. They have adjusted to the changes well, and Bob and his new wife and Kelly and I have all sort of come to terms with each other and are finding ways to communicate for the sake of our sons.

I am proud of Corey and Alex and who they have become, and deep down, I think they are proud of me. Together we met an enormous challenge, and we survived.

MY MUMMY IS FUNNY
Lynne D'Orsay

I am a 36-year-old Lesbian, of a rural New England white middle-class background. My daughter Hannah is six. I named her after my grandmother's grandmother, a strong woman who, widowed early, singlehandedly ran a large raspberry farm in Northern Maine in the late 1800s. I live in a New Hampshire seacoast city, with my lover and another Lesbian couple. My daughter lives with us half-time, as does the daughter of one of my housemates. Each of our children spends the other half of the week with her respective father.

I spent the first thirty years of my life trying very

hard, with occasional lapses, to be a "good girl," hoping to gain the approval of my parents. Throughout my childhood and adolescence, I had intensive friendships and attractions to other women, but assumed heterosexuality. At age nineteen, I began living with a man with whom I shared child-care responsibilities in an adolescent group home. We spent the next ten years together, achieving one "goal" after another — getting ourselves through college and vocational school, saving money, buying a house. During these ten years, despite my continuing strong attractions to and friendships with women, I remained in complete denial about my Lesbianism and out of touch with my internal misery at my way of life. I yearned for a child for several years before I got pregnant. Yet it was not long after my daughter's first birthday that I began my turbulent coming-out process. I can now see, looking back, that most of my efforts during my twenties went toward keeping myself emotionally numb and making myself acceptably female by becoming a nurse, a wife, and a mother. But once I had achieved all those notable landmarks of American womanhood, I found myself frustrated and unhappy. Years of introspection and self-examination followed, and during those same years, I was, as I am now, a mother. Never have I stopped loving my daughter with a totality that sometimes causes me joy, sometimes despair.

I can't talk about the process of coming out to my daughter without noting that it was thoroughly intertwined with my coming-out process to myself. I have a strong feeling that part of the reason I held back from coming out so long had to do with my desire for a daughter who I knew would be coming into my life someday, and my ignorance of other than a heterosexual model for mothering. I spent months, after acknowledging my Lesbianism, searching for some way to keep living my life as a straight woman. I dreaded the pain that speaking out about who I was would cause her; what disruptions would I cause to her young sweet life? My ultimate conclusion was that a childhood living with an unhappy mother, whose life was a lie, would harm her more than a marital break-up.

I now know this to be true, although there is no doubt that the divorce and the stress of having two homes have sometimes been very painful for her. Because I spent so long being closeted about my Lesbianism, as well as other aspects of myself, it has become very important to me to be as "out" as possible, while trying to skirt actual danger for myself and my child. I have been continuously advised by my daughter's other parents that my "flagrant" Lesbianism will harm her, embarrass her, cause concerns by her teachers, ruin her social life, lose her friends. I have given this a lot of thought. I have to believe that it is not me who is harming my child, but the homophobia of others, just as racism, sexism, ablism and all the other "isms" harm children in our culture. I choose to teach my daughter that we live in a culture that hates difference, but that difference is not a quality to be afraid of, and that it is ignorance that breeds this fear of Lesbians. Still, what do I do when she is teased in the playground for having a "Lezzie" for a mom? My first reaction is always to safeguard her, to hide for her, to protect her from this pain. I worry: where will her anger go? Can I help her move through it? Can I teach her my values? Or will she hate her mother and disavow all that she has been taught because of the pain it has caused her? I don't have the answers to these questions, so I continue to ponder it all and to mother in the way that feels right to me.

This brings up an aspect of my mothering which I feel is influenced by my Lesbianism. I voluntarily have joint custody of my daughter; in fact, she is with me less than three days a week. Her other parents (her father remarried when she was very young) have assumed the majority of the parental responsibility in most aspects of her life. Partly, it is because of the ambivalence I feel about the pain that my Lesbianism might cause her which makes joint custody preferable to me. I recognize that one of the luxuries of my situation is that my daughter has one life with straight parents in one town, and a different life in a non-traditional Lesbian family in another. There is little overlap between these lives, and I think that each family can serve as a pressure-valve release for the other. In her other family, Hannah can feel "normal" with married heterosexual parents, a dose of traditional religion and mainstream mores. In my family, with four adult Lesbian caretakers, she finds a feminist consciousness, a questioning attitude and flexible rules, as well as an acknowledgement of and pride in our difference. I think that my daughter is aware at an early age that there are many ways to live, that choices can be made, that there is not just one "right" way. Because of these factors, I never really stopped to face the decision that many Lesbians do — shall I come out to my child? Being a Lesbian is so much of who I am that I could not question whether I would let my daughter know that I was a

Lesbian, any more than I would try to hide from her that I am a woman.

I struggle to express these seldom-spoken feelings. I love my daughter intensely. I remember when she was an infant of six months or so. A fly landed on her beautiful face, and I felt a surge of anger pulse through me as intense as any feeling in my life, that anything could dare sully this child I loved so much. And yet, emotions persist concurrently; I am sometimes a half-hearted mother, a mother who freely admits that I do not want to be a mother more than three days a week; and sometimes even that can feel like too much. Although I have not resolved my guilt about my maternal ambivalence, I am sure that my daughter gets the best of me with the arrangement I have now. I can best give her the love and attention she needs when I have a portion of the week to devote to my lover, my friends, myself and my work. I see the potential in me for being the spiteful, angry mother my mother was if I were mothering full-time. It is only in the Lesbian community that I feel I am given the space to question my feelings about motherhood while I am in fact mothering. By straight women, I am quickly cast as unnatural and alien if I voice these feelings.

Probably because I have always been out to my daughter, she seems easy and comfortable with my Lesbianism. I want to emphasize that I appreciate the factors which have allowed me to be out to my daughter from a young age. When I talk to Lesbian mothers who are not out to their children, or who come out later in their lives, I am struck by the amount of energy used in keeping the secret, and I wonder whether later in life their children will be

153

angry with them precisely because of this concealment. I remember finding out in my twenties that my mother had clandestinely been running her father's business after his death for many years. How I would have liked to know that my mother was functioning as a competent businesswoman! And how I scorned her at that time for needing to keep her strength and intelligence a secret!

Staying closeted for the children's sake does seem to have some potential problems to me. Should a child be allowed to believe she has the power to define her parent? Do we want to surrender to our children — out of fear — the power to say "I don't want you to be who you are, so don't be who you are in front of me or anyone else"? Will the child perceive that her parent doesn't like herself/himself enough to show the child her or his real self? Will the child be confused by her seeming power to "decide" who her parent really is? As painful as the homophobia of our culture will be for our children, I think the confused identity message that we give our children if we stay in the closet to them can be even more detrimental.

Another aspect of Lesbian parenting I would like to see addressed is the child's grandparents' reaction to the parent as homosexual. In my case, when I came out to my parents when Hannah was three, they immediately disowned me and my daughter. We have had no contact with them for three years now. Along with the many facets I've considered about being disowned, I have worried about how this reaction to my Lesbianism has influenced Hannah. For the first year, hoping that my parents would come around, I didn't discuss it with her. But

154

eventually I had to explain why there were no more birthday cards, Christmas presents, or Sunday visits to her grandparents and cousins. I have told her that it has nothing to do with her, that it is between my parents and me, that what they have done is sad and wrong, and that it is not anything I would ever do to her, no matter who she "becomes." Sometimes I have the tendency to be too passive about the cruelties of homophobia as just something that "happens" to us — thus at first I had a hard time getting angry at being disowned myself, but found it easier to become enraged about how my parents have treated their granddaughter.

Still, watching my daughter as she lives her days in the open way that children do, I cannot help but believe that I have done the right thing. I hope "Lesbian Mother Vignettes" like these will become a commonplace of American life:

One Halloween, a neighbor asks my daughter, "and what are you tonight?" "A cat," she answers. "And what's your mommy?" "Oh, she's a dyke," shouts my four-year-old daughter over her shoulder as she runs off toward the next house.

Our daughters, five and six, are playing house together in the attic. We hear their voices come wafting down the stairs. "Let's pretend we're all grown up and we're Lesbians and we live together and share all our crystals!" they say enthusiastically. But thirty minutes later we're likely to hear them negotiating who is going to be "the daddy" and who "the mommy." I love how they try on future roles, like hats. When asked what she intends to be when she grows up, my daughter is as likely to answer "an amazon" as "a ballerina" or, once, "a pigeon."

Our two daughters are playing with a tea set. We hear them say excitedly, "Let's play Lesbian-feminist brunch." These are the same children who love to traipse around the house wearing white tablecloths and singing "Here Comes The Bride."

"I don't want to be a Lesbian when I grow up because I want to wear a bra," says my friend's daughter. I have to pull up my shirt to convince her that I, a bona fide Lesbian, often wear a bra. (She is very impressed that I own "a silky one.")

Best of all, just the other day I hear my daughter saying proudly to her kindergarten friends, "I told you my mummy is funny, she thinks different from other people."

POEM TO MY SON
VISITING HIS FATHER
Esther Hawk

If I told you sometimes she holds me
the way I hold you, that we swim

as if the water were home
and we had no memory of air,

and when I say I love her, will you know
this is a secret, even though it shouldn't be.

THE SECRETS OUR CHILDREN KEEP FOR US
Heather Wishik

A law school classmate and I fell in love. We both had sons, mine just three and hers a year older. We were both from the East and felt like uneasy transplants in California. We both had Jewish family backgrounds. We both hated coffee and drank tea. But there was a difference. Her divorce was already final. She had been blackmailed into agreeing to burdensome visitation arrangements and too little money because her ex knew she had had an affair with a woman. I was more naive: my divorce was pending and my spouse, who was then living across the country, had no information with which to hurt me, yet, but a custody battle terrified me. My classmate and I remained best friends, babysat for each other, shared meals and nursed each other through the illnesses brought on by the exhaustion of single parenting, law school, and employment. At her insistence, and with my agreement, we never became sexual. This was torture for both of us. A few months before my law school graduation my soon-to-be-ex spouse backed down and signed a settlement giving me sole custody. But nothing changed for my friend. I moved away as soon as I graduated. Within less than a year she remarried.

Two years later I began an affair with a woman who lived far from my new home and only occasionally came into town. Before she stayed at my house overnight I decided I'd best talk with my son. I invited him to breakfast at our favorite cafe. At age five going out to breakfast and being allowed to eat pancakes with maple syrup was one of the biggest treats he could imagine.

During breakfast I told him that some grown-up women love men, and some love other women. I told him some people didn't think women should love other women, or men other men, and that who a person loved was, I believed, their own business, and private. I told him I had met a very special woman whom I loved a lot and that she was going to come visit us. I said she was also a poet, that she had

159

children, including two sons, and that I thought he would like her. And I explained that she loved me.

He asked me where she was going to sleep: kids are nothing if not direct. I told him in my bed with me. He asked if he could sleep there too. I said no. He was quiet for a while. He asked her name. While we were walking back to our car he took my hand and said, "Mommy, I'm glad you found somebody. I know it's been a long time since you had anybody to love you and you've been lonely. And I think people are stupid who say it's not all right."

The following year my then current lover gave my son a special hat. He collected hats and was thrilled by the gift. A few weeks later he was sitting on the floor packing a suitcase for a visit with his father, whom he had not seen for more than a year. He packed the special hat. I sat down on the floor and gathered him into my lap. "If daddy asks where you got the hat, what will you tell him?" I asked. "Jennifer gave it to me." "And if he asks who Jennifer is, what will you say?" I continued. "I'll tell him she's our friend." By this point he was looking at me quizzically.

"Do you remember I told you some people don't think women should love other women?" "Yes." I hugged him. "I'm afraid your Dad might be one of those people. He might think it's not o.k. for you to grow up in a house with a mother who loves other women. And if he thought that, he might decide it would be better for you to go live with him. He wouldn't do it to be mean, but just because he loves you and really might think it would be bad for you to grow up with me. And he might be able to persuade a judge he was right, because lots of judges

160

are mixed up about these things and think women who love other women aren't good mothers."

My son was looking frightened. "You're a good mother. And I want to live with you."

"I know. Anyway, I need you to keep it a secret, my loving other women. It's not something your Dad needs to know. And I'm worried if you bring the hat and he asks you questions it will be hard for you to answer without his finding out Jennifer is my lover. You can bring it if you can think of a way to explain getting it that won't let him know."

"I think I'll leave my hat at home."

When my son was eight I began the relationship I am still in. The relationship remained a secret from most people for the first year because of our work situations. My son was aware of our secrecy, of how we did not go to public places together. When we stayed at her house we put my car into the garage so it would not be seen in the yard by colleagues who drove past. The garage was really a small barn, and my son pretended we were playing the "Dukes of Hazard" hiding the vehicle in the barn. One day at my house my son and I were playing.

PLAYTIME

You are eight. We are seated on the kitchen floor
taking turns arranging letter magnets
on the fridge, spelling out who it is we love
like carvings on trees, or like bathroom graffiti.
You spell I LOVE GRANDMA. I spell I LOVE
    SUSAN
and you change it to WE. Then you say
"Someone might see it" and you change it

161

to WE LOVE AMERICA. "There," you tell me,
"now no one will know what we really mean."

You asked once "Will they send you
to jail if they find out you're a lesbian?"
and I reassured you I'd only lose my job.
Now, sitting on the floor playing with you
I feel a crowd gathering, your long-gone
father and the rest who feel some right
to be here, to tell me who to be, or worse,
to take you away. And it is losing you
that I am suddenly sitting on the floor
crying about, this is the danger
I cannot explain when you ask why the tears.

Seven years later my son is, by his own choice,
living in another country with his Dad and visiting
me. I had always told him that when he was older he
could live with his Dad if he wanted to and if his
Dad agreed. When he turned 13 my son decided he
wanted to know his Dad better. At first he went for
just one school year, but since then he and I have
agreed it's working fine and he'll stay through high
school.

He is almost 15 now and has still never said
anything to his father about my lesbianism.
Apparently there are often lectures about how terrible
being gay is. My son tells me he refuses to engage in
these conversations. And he tells me he thinks his
Dad is really stupid about these things. "I can't wait
'till I'm grown up and can tell him what I really
think about it. I'm going to tell him being a lesbian
has nothing to do with whether you are a good
mother." But he also tells me he is afraid of living in

my house again, because I am now very visible publicly as a lesbian: "The kids in school, they think all gays have A.I.D.S.: if they knew you were a lesbian they'd definitely give me a hard time." He's probably right.

ELI AND I
Marcia Diane

My son was born February 19, 1970 at 4:25 a.m.
His father took him outside and held him up to be
baptized by the stars. Several hours later he told me
he had had a vision before the child was born that
we would have a son and his name would be Eli.
This is true. I was 26 years old and had never even
heard the word Lesbian.

Right after I wrote this paragraph I had to stop
and wait until I talked to Eli. This was very hard for
me because I was terrifically excited about writing for
the anthology. I really couldn't continue until I asked

him if I could use his name. If I didn't ask, it would be coming out for him. No one has the right to come out for someone else.

When we finally talked about the article he said: "It will really be something no matter which way I decide, won't it?" I agreed that this was so. If he told me not to use his name, I would certainly honor his request; that means he matters and how he feels matters. If he said I could use his name, that means he is willing to take the risk of coming out in print. Considering Eli is eighteen and has not shared that his mom is a Lesbian with any of his friends yet, this is quite a chance for him to take. Two days later when we were out to pizza together, he said I could use his name. Wow, was I proud! He had taken a giant step toward owning his heritage.

I also talked to my lover-mate, Ellen, about the article, to check on using her name and also to get feedback. I kept thinking in terms of writing my coming out story. Ellen said this made perfect sense to her. Coming out to ourselves is often how we tell our children.

As soon as I began work on this story a great deal of pain resurfaced . . . so much that I was unable to continue working on it. Being gay is painful for all of us, but I am just beginning to understand how painful it is for our children.

A good way through my pain and stuckness is to share with friends. So I began to tell others what I was struggling against. One night at our friend's house a story was told by one of the women about how her mother said she never wanted her to come home again after she shared with her mother that she was a Lesbian. My heart ached for her, but it set me free to write again. I would never tell my son not to come home again.

Eli was twelve when I divorced his father. Soon thereafter I fell in love with a woman who was with another. That did not stop us; we just decided to have a threesome. It was joyous, raucous, passionate, and filled with pain and abandonment. Though this affair was doomed to failure, it was with these women that I truly became initiated into the Lesbian culture and became woman-identified. They took me to parties, events, and political rallies, where always the thrust was woman-centered women, women loving women. I loved it. I blossomed in this atmosphere. It felt like coming home. There was, however, one place it did pinch. More and more it became apparent that male children over ten or twelve, sometimes even eight, were not welcome at these gatherings. I felt incensed, and at the same moment was grateful that Eli was not with me, that he was at his friend's house or with his dad or down at Gramma's. In this way, I managed to avoid dealing with this very painful reality.

About a year after the threesome relationship ended, I joined a Lesbian support group. Gradually one of the members and I realized we were attracted to each other. That was my girl Ellen. We spent long hours on the flower-strewn hills of Sonoma County rationalizing why we couldn't be lovers. One of the big reasons was that about six months previously Ellen had ended a lover relationship with a woman who had an eight-year-old daughter. This had caused enormous pain for Ellen because she also had to give up her relationship with the child. She did not want to begin a new relationship with another lover's child. I truly respected how she felt, and she respected my concern that my son was part of my life. Here at last was the place I was to confront the issue of my son being accepted by my culture.

Once again, the Goddess gave me the space I needed to make sense out of my life. Eli announced that he was going to go live with his dad. This gave Ellen's and my relationship the year it needed to become solid. The following summer Eli came home for his summer visit with us and announced that he could not go back. His father was continuing to be abusive toward him and it seemed to be getting worse despite the fact that they were in therapy together. Without a second thought, Ellen and I said Eli could stay.

We all tried our best, each of us displaying the most exemplary behavior. Ellen did her best to be a step- or co-parent. I did my best as a mom in her first Lesbian relationship that had any stability. Eli did his fifteen-year-old best. He was too good to be true. His self-appointed job was to not be a fifteen-year-old sexually active heterosexual male living with two dykes. It was a hard job we all had. We were extremely uncomfortable. We moved. Surely a bigger house with more separate space would help. It didn't. The pretending got worse. At last we sat down to talk about what was not working. Ellen and I needed a home alone. We needed desperately to have a home without males. Ellen was constitutionally incapable of taking care of her own needs in the face of the needs of children because of having raised her five brothers and sisters at her own expense. I felt on the brink of being able to bond for the first time ever with a person equal to me in a lover relationship, and I was terrified. Eli needed a home where adolescent male was A-OK. He needed permission to be who he was and have his needs met, and Ellen and I were failing miserably at that task. Ellen worked with her therapist, and I worked with mine. We had more meetings together, hoping the pain would resolve itself, hoping it would go away. It didn't. We finally came down to Ellen and me getting separate accommodations or Eli leaving. Everyone was stunned. We all hurt. There did not appear to be any winning here. To make matters more painful, my therapist declared that I would ruin Eli if he were to not live with me. Then the miracle started to happen. We all started to share our feelings. We got real and there with each other. Eli had permission to be angry at us and hate us. I had permission to say I could not do parenting any more the way he needed it, and Ellen got to say she wanted to continue to have a relationship with him. Miracles every one filled with joy and pain.

One day Eli and I were alone driving for one of his practice drives so he could pass his driving test for his license. We began to talk about the choices before us. I said if I chose him over Ellen, it would be putting the burden on him to be "acting" as my lover and I did not want that. He told me he felt this was true and he did not want or need the burden. I think it was at this point that we both knew what we needed to do. A month before Eli turned sixteen, he moved in with a family friend.

Though these times were painful and often felt permanently grim, we did have lighter moments. One day Ellen and I returned home from work to find our bulletin board purged of all "offensive Lesbo materials." Eli's friends had been over and he had taken it down in order to "pass." At first when we talked with him about this, he seemed acutely embarrassed. Finally we were all reduced to laughter as we shared "passing as an art form" stories. It was a warm moment for us all. A common bond was beginning to develop between us, a sort of conspiracy together, a sense of belonging to this other culture, us by sexual-affectional preference, Eli by relation. In a way, we are bi-cultural.

It was in the latter part of his seventeenth year that Eli was able to express his discomfort with my being a Lesbian. He told Ellen and me that he was just not comfortable being seen in public with us because we were queer. Ellen and I knew that Eli would have to experience this homophobia at some point. We all do. We totally supported how he felt and reassured him that we would not now or ever come out for him. I believe this set Eli quite at ease. We are from a small town, and Eli has been raised here all his life. He has high stakes. We drew the line at him and his friends making "queer jokes" or derogatory remarks about gays in our presence. This was really put to the test when Eli and I returned from an outing in San Francisco. His friends were all gathered on the sidewalk as we drove up to his house. They began joking around with him about who he had met in the bathrooms. Eli shot a glance at me and then at his friends. The joking abruptly ceased. It was an incredible feeling to see those adolescent boys, whom I had known since grade school, put it together so fast on that sunny afternoon sidewalk. They were putting down their best friend's mom, and that just wasn't OK with them. Warm goodbyes were passed all around as usual when I drove off, and I felt as if a small miracle had happened.

In September of 1987 Ellen and I decided to get married. We planned a ceremony to be held in the park. We were married by a minister from the Church of Natural Grace, a church which was affiliated with a psychic healing institute. We invited most of our friends in the community and a few relatives. Neither of our parents would attend. My brother and mother are dead, so I felt very strongly about Eli attending. We invited him, and he said he would have to think it over. To attend an openly gay wedding of your mother right at the height of your rejecting gayness totally was asking a lot.

The ceremony included many excerpts from Judy Grahn's work *Gay Words Gay Worlds*. It was so validating to hear these words spoken out loud in a public place in front of the Goddess and everyone, proclaiming our right to exist, our right to our culture, as all other minorities have.

Eli did attend our wedding and took full part in the huge circle ceremony. We were all so proud and excited. We had sports and games after the ceremony. Eli and I spent the majority of time on the lake, he wind surfing and I canoeing. I guess we needed that space. He found that he had many friends there. He was happy to see the women whom he had voluntarily chosen to live with in Santa Rosa, a totally Lesbian household. They all loved him to pieces and found him to be a totally charming young man.

The child had come full circle to become a young man. He decided to take his savings and go to

Europe instead of college. Ellen and I applauded his choice to go play. He has worked incredibly hard and has earned every penny to spend on himself as he chooses. Though I never had to say to my son, "Honey, there's something I've been meaning to tell you," he has had to live every minute of the joy, the agony, the pain, and triumph that each of us must walk through. He did it like a man, even while yet a child. I am proud of each of us for our willingness to struggle to be honest and to share our love. As far as I can see, it just won't stop.

Author's Note: I've read, reread, and editorialized this story over and over, striving always for some quality which kept eluding me. Finally I have found the element missing. The story seems devoid of feeling. It reads very centered on self: me. I don't like that fact. I wish to rewrite it again and again, until I can get it to sing and be magical, get it shiny and inspirational. But I believe now that I must own it as is, own its awkwardness and pain, its small glimmerings of hope and joy. This is how it was for Eli and me. I might wish it different, but the greatest gift for him and me is to accept it. From the acceptance comes a solid foundation, like the first fort he built at age eleven: Sinking four solid piers into the ground, he built a structure that stood strong. This story is true. In its truth we can stand strong and build whatever kind of tomorrow we choose.

—M. Diane
—June 1988

LOVE COMES
IN MANY FORMS
Terry Love

In 1979, I came out to my two sons, who were then 9 and 10 years old.

At that time I belonged to a Black Lesbian support group. During a discussion on coming out, a teacher shared how she had come out to her daughter. My lover and I discussed it; we decided to have my sons and me come to dinner at my lover's apartment and then we'd all talk.

As my lover was clearing the table and washing the dishes, I launched into my prepared speech. I had

172

cut out paper dolls, two large males and two small ones, and two large females and two small ones. I held up two dolls in each hand.

"Love comes in many forms: girls and boys, men and women" — changing the dolls — "two boys, two girls, two men, two women. You have girl friends and boy friends. And you have your best friend." They both nodded, accepted the paper dolls, and began playing with them.

Marilyn came out of the kitchen and stood beside me. "What your mother is trying to say is that she and I are lovers and we are all four going to live together."

My younger son Frank threw down the paper dolls and stood up. "Not with my mother you don't!" he stormed, and stalked off to the living room. I asked John, "What do you think?" He smiled and said, "Whatever makes you happy, Mom."

Over the next few months, Marilyn wooed, bribed, and tried to ingratiate herself with Frank. She took him to the children's museum at the Art Institute. We took both boys skating in Lincoln Park. We tried everything. Frank never changed his mind.

Eight years later, Frank is the one who gets along well with my current lover. He respects and looks up to her. John left after one year — irreconcilable differences.

WHY I WRITE
ANONYMOUSLY
A. W.

I tried to find out from my kids what it was like
to have a mother who is a lesbian, but I didn't get
much info. Their basic message was that it was okay
with them as long as their friends never found out.
So, my lover is my sister and their aunt. And
everything is cool.

* * * * *

Back in 1980 my friend Nancy and I and my kids Alexandria, Tyrone, and Ellen were returning from the National Women's Music Festival in Champaign. I had come out to myself two years before. The lover of my housemate, who frequently visited from out of state, was very political. The kids had overheard (although they did not understand) much feminist, and some separatist, theory.

I am a relatively short woman, 5 feet and 1.5 inches to be exact. About a year earlier my best friend, who is just under 5 feet, and myself decided that short people were greatly denigrated in our culture. We founded a group with a brief and informal membership called Micromorphs of Milwaukee. We had a party and nailed a board across the front door at 5 feet 3 inches. If you couldn't walk under it without bending your knees, you couldn't come to the party. At any rate, we were all driving through the flat Illinois cornfields and Nancy and I were discussing Joan, who is definitely not a micromorph, but definitely is a lesbian.

As we drove through the Illinois cornfields, Nancy and I were discussing Joan and lesbian-separatist politics. The conversation had gone on for several minutes when a firm seven-year-old voice came from the back seat, "Joan isn't a lesbian."

Stunned silence filled the front seat. "What do you mean, Ellen?" I asked.

"She can't be. She's too tall."

It took me a few moments to realize that the words lesbian and micromorph were interchangeable in her mind, and that meant she didn't really know what either meant.

* * * * *

I don't remember the first time my kids heard the word lesbian, and they don't remember either. They were 5, 6 and 7 when I began to apply the word to myself, and by then their father and I were divorced. This word referred to something that was not important in their young lives. As they grew, other things that made them different from their friends were probably more pressing, but even these things were so much a part of their normal lives that they were not conscious issues of childhood. The three kids are all adopted. They have always known this. They are all of different brown skin heritages; both their parents are white. As young children most of their friends were like them, and our neighborhood contained many other families like ours, as far as racial identity and adoption went. The divorce created more differences than race or adoption.

Now they are teens, and they seem to have done pretty well with all of this. They more often have to explain away a white parent or their humorous last name than they do their race or their mother's sexuality. As Tyrone says, "It's cool with me, as long as my friends don't know." And that's the bottom line for them; don't let their friends know.

For the past seven years I have been living with my lover, Stephanie. Alex, my oldest, was eleven when Stephanie moved in. I asked all three of them first

how they felt about it, and they all agreed —
whatever their private thoughts were. I remember
what Tyrone, then ten, said. "It's okay, Mom, because
she makes you happy." And this from the kid that
never got along with Stephanie.

Alex always seemed to have the most trouble with
my lesbianism. She has always been precocious in her
awareness of my sexuality. She is the one who
reacted if I said another woman was good looking,
who caught the looks between Stephanie and me, who
suspected why we took afternoon naps. And she is
the one who grabbed onto the invention of Stephanie
as her aunt. Now she had a valid explanation for this
other woman who lived in her house, and who acted
parental towards her. Stephanie was her aunt,
Stephanie's kids her cousins. Even when she and
Stephanie went to the Michigan Women's Music
Festival, Stephanie was her aunt. "Why do you call
me aunt here?" asked Stephanie. "Nobody here
cares."

"I don't know," she responded. And persisted.

Even at home, where most of the neighbors know,
it is Aunt Stephanie. I said to her once, "You know,
Alex, you are just making problems for yourself. What
do you think Anita thought when you said Stephanie
was your aunt? She knows about Stephanie and me."

"No, she doesn't. How could she!"

"Because I know John knows, because your father
told him, and I have never pretended it's not true.
And I am sure he has told others. But do you think
they care? They are as friendly with me as they ever
were. They invite me to neighborhood gatherings.

Alex, these people are too liberal to admit to prejudice around this. They may be uncomfortable, but they will never do or say anything bad."

But I don't think Alexandria believed me. She once told me that if her friends at school were to find out, she could never go back there. She said, "You don't know how teenagers are. They always make fun of kids they think are gay. They think being gay is terrible. They would never talk to me again."

I then named one of her best friends who I think knows and doesn't care, a young woman now in college, a couple of years older than Alex. "She doesn't know," said Alex.

"Are you sure?"

"We never talk about it."

When Alex was 13 and 14 she always maintained that the boys around her were just friends, nothing special. Not boyfriends. The summer she was to turn 15 I finally broached the subject directly. We were driving through the countryside and I said, "It's okay with me for you to like boys, to have boyfriends. I always expected you to have boyfriends. The fact that I am a lesbian doesn't make you one, nor do I expect you or want you to be one. I want you to do, be, what is right for you. You might be straight all your life, you might be straight for awhile and then be with women, or vice versa. Things like this can change. People try out different ways of relating." I told her of a woman she knew as a lesbian who is now married and a mother. She seemed to be reassured by all this. Perhaps it was that I would accept her choices for herself, or perhaps she had been worried on some level that if I was a lesbian she would automatically be one too. She seemed to need to hear this, and she began to admit she liked boys.

I think one aspect of this which was hard for the kids was their father's reaction. I know that he called me a man-hater, used lesbian as a dirty word, and called me a castrating bitch — all in their hearing. During the early years I stressed that although it was okay to be a lesbian, I didn't want them to tell other people, especially their father. (I was afraid of a custody suit.) What effect this double message has had I don't know.

Ellen submitted, unwillingly, to the following interview:

Me: How has it been, having a lesbian as a mother?
E: Normal. (Pause.) I don't know.
Me: Are you afraid to have your friends know?
E: Yeah.
Me: Why? How would they react?
E: I don't know. (Said quickly and loudly.)
Me: You don't know. What do you think?
E: I don't know. (Even more emphatically.)
Me: You afraid they wouldn't like you anymore?
E: Yeah.
Me: Even Yolanda?
E: Yeah. All of them.
Me: You're probably right. Do you remember when you first really knew what the word lesbian meant? You heard it before you understood it.
E: No.

* * * * *

Once we were all having hamburgers in a local gay bar. Alex, then about 11, looked around and asked why men were only sitting with men, and women with women. I told her it was a gay bar. She, looking very concerned, asked if it was okay for her to be there, as "I'm straight."

* * * * *

Coming out to my kids is the least of our problems. Right now its the stress of a constantly changing family size. Me, Stephanie, Ellen equal 3. Then there's Amy and Joey, Stephanie's grandkids, who live with us most of the time. And sometimes her teen, Andy, when he's back from school. So that's 5 to 8, depending. Plus her eldest, his wife and their 2-year-old are here for a while now, until they have surfaced from debt and can move out. So today it's 8, but can be up to 11, plus Amy and Joey's mother comes at holidays, to make 12.

We are out to all these people, if only because we only have so many beds! The hardest person of all these to come out to was Sean, Stephanie's adult son. She was scared and made me hide upstairs. But he said, "Hey Mom, it's okay. Whatever you want is fine." And he meant it. Her mom, who is like a mom to me, is the hardest. We think she knows, but the risk feels too high to tell.

THE TRUTH IS . . .
Jeri Broxterman

1

"It's tough when you're nine. Mom and Dad don't seem to be getting along too well lately. I don't know what the problem is but I do know that their arguing scares me," thinks my oldest daughter. But she says nothing.

I know I have to talk to Jonell about this. It's just not fair to her or to me for her to see the effect and not know the cause. At least if I talk to her first, maybe she won't suffer remorse later for the awful things that can be said in a moment of hurt and anger.

Jonell and I had a good relationship, and since she was born when I was 18 without the benefit of marriage, I had felt obligated to give her a little briefing on society. I told her that society had certain rules that people were supposed to follow, and one of them was that women were to marry first and have children second. It didn't take her long to deduce that her mother had done things in a little different order than the norm. After having laid this groundwork several years previously, I felt that I just might have an advantage when it came time for the coming-out story.

I found a quiet time to sit and talk. I chose my words carefully and reminded her of society's rules. Sometimes people are different, sometimes people just do not fit into molds. Your mother is different, I said. I told her as carefully as I could that I had fallen in love with a woman and that I had to face the fact that I was gay. She needed to know that I had not changed in my love for her.

I told Jonell that I was not the least bit ashamed of my sexuality and that she should not be either. I felt like such a traitor having to say to her to keep this hush hush, but I knew how cruel young people can be. I did not want my child hurt by other people's ignorance.

Just as I began to feel at a loss for words, Jonell rescued me, saying something that I will never forget. Smiling, she looked me in the eye and said, "Mom, I always knew you liked girls, I just didn't know there was a name for it!"

2

My son John was another matter. He always had a mind of his own. Got his stubbornness from his mother.

He was about seven when he started noticing that his mother was not exactly like his friends' mothers. John had been known to excitedly proclaim, "I'm really lucky because I have two mommies, most kids only have one mommy." Of course, my lover Carol and I never hesitated to agree with him in this matter; two mommies were certainly better than one.

The social prejudice began to surface when he reached elementary school. Again, John was not exactly quiet about his abundance of mommies. Before long my ex-husband found himself being asked some rather personal questions at a parent/teacher conference. "Does your wife live here in town?" Yes. "Does she live with someone?" Yes, her roommate. "Are they just roommates? No, they are not. "Well, that certainly explains what John is talking about!"

Because I did not have principal custody of my children (we had shared parenting), I did not get the benefit of attending that parent/teacher conference and voicing my disapproval of that insensitive, homophobic teacher.

One day while attending a festival in the park, John proved he had been paying attention when I had told him that if he ever felt he was lost, he should go to the nearest police officer. After getting separated from us in the crowd, he went up to the police officers and told them, "I'm here with my two mommies, one is this big and one is this big." With a description like that, it didn't take us long to be reunited.

3

I do not know if I ever came out to my youngest daughter. Jodi was so little when I knew I had to leave that her innocence could not be shattered by adult truths like prejudice. Jodi would happily sit on my lover Carol's lap, quietly sucking her thumb and twirling Carol's curls around her finger.

4

Many things have happened since I came out and left my children in the trust and care of my ex-husband. He remarried; his wife's father sexually molested my daughters; the twisted court system, seeing my sexual preference as a perversion, arrested me. Jonell, John and Jodi were forced by their stepmother to say bad things against their bad Mommy. They were too afraid not to. The man I chose to represent me used knowledge of my sexual preference in an attempt to discourage me from a jury trial. He assured me that the Judge and Jury would see the abuse that my Jonell and Jodi suffered as a rite of passage in making little lesbians. My ignorance and fear convinced me that I would never receive a fair trial. I pled no contest, was adjudicated guilty and sent to prison.

As a final blow, the Judge ordered that I have no contact with my children for the next 12-1/2 years.

So you see, I do not know how my children have fared from my confession of love for another woman.

184

I can only hope and pray that they possess the strength to find out the truth for themselves and love me, as I have loved them.

V
THE POLITICS
OF COMING OUT:
ISSUES AND PROBLEMS

As important as coming out can be for family relationships, it is even more important in a larger arena — that of politics. Because coming out to one's children is an issue that has not been very fully explored, many political and legal questions remain unanswered. We need a great deal more data than we have on how coming out affects our relationships with our children. In some states it can affect whether or not we can retain custody of our children. It can determine whether we will live with our lovers or not. It can affect the closeness and honesty of our relationships with the rest of our families; few aspects of Lesbian and gay lives are wholly unaffected by our relationships with our children. This section explores some of those questions and offers some tentative legal and political suggestions.

At the same time, coming out represents the possibility of imagining and creating genuine alternative family structures and breaking down traditional sex roles. In a very real sense, our

187

openness with our children affects everyone's perceptions of the nature of the family, for as we make gay and Lesbian families visible we expand the social services available to our children. All this points to the need for us to come out *as families* as well as to our children.

Ultimately, coming out to our children is the first step in understanding the political and cultural artifact that heterosexuality is. If all Lesbian and gay parents were to come out fully to their children and their families, it would be the beginning of a radical change in Western culture, which divides and judges people on the basis of sexual orientation. We might indeed create a truly free family.

TO TELL OR NOT TO TELL:
Some Legal Implications of Coming Out to Children
Heather R. Wishik, Esq.*

For lesbians or gay men who desire to have a
continuing relationship in the form of visitation or
custody with their children, coming out to anyone, let
alone coming out to those children, is legally very
risky. Assuming the gay or lesbian parent is the
child's only biological parent, the risks of coming out

---

*This article is a general discussion only and does not
constitute legal advice. A person with specific custody or visitation
problems should see an attorney for advice. All information
contained herein represents 1988 or earlier rulings.

are narrower: intervention by a close relative, such as a grandparent, or by a social services agency claiming the parent is abusing or neglecting the child, are both possible, and relatives have been provoked to seek custody when a parent reveals a homosexual identity. However, the lesbian and gay parents most at risk are those whose children have another living biological parent who is straight. It is in the latter situations that, unless the parents come to their own agreement, courts have to choose between placing children in a straight or a gay or lesbian household. Courts in these situations also have the option to place the child with the straight parent *and* drastically restrict the visitation rights of the lesbian or gay parent.

Most custody and visitation matters involving two living parents are settled by agreement of the parents, which agreements are then ratified by a court if there is a legal proceeding such as divorce going on. In an increasing number of states, parental agreements as to custody are presumed to be in children's best interests and courts cannot overrule them without cause. Thus, for gay and lesbian parents whose children have a second biological parent involved, agreements as to custody and visitation may avoid handing the issue of parental homosexuality to a judge for decision. However, no court order, based upon an agreement or otherwise, relating to the welfare of children, is ever really final. That is, such orders are subject to later modification if the party seeking a change can demonstrate a change of circumstances or similar basis. This means that a parent who keeps her or his identity secret from the other parent during initial custody or visitation proceedings risks having a later modification proceeding brought based upon newly discovered information about sexual orientation.

For those parents who cannot or will not remain celibate and closeted, it often seems to make sense to try to keep information about sexual orientation from the straight parent. Part of this effort sometimes means hiding one's identity from the children: sometimes it means asking the children to keep the secret with you. Most children will not succeed in this endeavor, so having the information the other parent does not know in the children's hands is like a time bomb waiting to go off. It is also a no-win choice: that is, children surprised during a custody or visitation battle by the information that a parent is gay or straight understandably may react negatively. Thus a parent wishing to minimize the possibly negative emotional impact of the information may want to give it to their child themselves in a non-crisis and loving setting. However, a parent who does so risks having a judge feel that the parent has negatively impacted the child's moral development by coming out to the child. And for parents who are out to their children, having any other lesbians or gay men in the home, especially for overnight visits, or taking the children to any events, social or political, in which other lesbians and gay men participate, can make the legal situation worse, even though it is exactly such contact with other gay people, and their children, which may best assist the children in adjusting to their parent's gay or lesbian identity.

The legal system at its worst wants no lesbian or gay parents to have custody, and wants gay or lesbian visiting parents to hide their identity from their

191

children, or at least not to "practice homosexuality" around their children. To many courts this means no other lesbians or gay men around, no gay events, no lesbian literature or politics, no discussions with the kids. Virginia and Missouri fall into this category. In Virginia, the state supreme court has ruled that homosexual parents are unfit as a matter of law: no examination of a gay or lesbian parent's actual parenting skills is needed before a court can remove a child from that parent's custody. [*Roe v. Roe*, 324 SE2d 691 (1985)]. In Missouri, a series of appellate court decisions between 1980 and the present have concluded that, in order to protect "the moral growth and best interests" of children, and to protect them from "peer pressure, teasing, and possible ostracizing they may encounter as a result of the 'alternative life style' their [parent] has chosen," children must be removed from the custody of lesbian or gay parents, at least if those parents are in a relationship with anyone and allow anyone in the community to be aware of their orientation. [*S.E.G. v. R.A.G.*, (Mo. Ct. App. EDist. 7/21/87) (13 FLR 1497), citing *J.L.P.(H.) v. D.J.P.*, 643 S.W.2d 865 (Mo. App., W.D. 1982); *L. v. D.*, 630 S.W.2d 240 (Mo. App., S.D. 1982); *N.K.M. v. L.E.M.*, 606 S.W.2d 179 (Mo. App., W.D. 1980)].

In general, states in the south and midwest have been the most negative toward gay and lesbian parents' rights. This is not, however, uniformly true. In a recent South Carolina decision the state Court of Appeals refused to remove children from the custody of a lesbian mother after she began a relationship with another woman: the father was seeking a change in custody several years after the original divorce custody order. This father knew at the time of the original divorce that the mother was a lesbian, but did not raise it at that time. The South Carolina Court of Appeals held that homosexuality does not make a parent automatically unfit, and that the husband's prior knowledge meant there had not been a sufficient change of circumstances since the divorce to modify custody simply based upon the mother's having begun a lesbian relationship. However, the court also reviewed the substantive evidence of the children's adjustment, concluding there was no evidence that the lesbian relationship had adversely affected the children "in any substantial way." [*Stroman v. Williams,* (S.Ca.Ct.App. 2/23/87) (13 FLR 1182)].

The rationale used by the South Carolina court is called the "nexus test": the theory is that an aspect of parental identity or behavior, including homosexuality, should not have a bearing upon custody or visitation decisions unless it can be shown adversely to affect the children. The problem with this test is that, as can be seen in the Missouri cases discussed above, if a judge wants to find an adverse effect on the children one can be found, even if it is only a possible future effect based upon possible peer pressures or social disapprobation.

The reported facts in the South Carolina case do not include how long the mother had been out to her children before she began living with another woman. Whatever her choices were about coming out to the children, by the time the father attempted to take custody the evidence showed that the children were "properly adjusted," in the words of the court. The *Stroman v. Williams* case is encouraging because it indicates that if the lesbian or gay custodian is able to demonstrate that the children are o.k., both in terms of their own development and in terms of their adjustment to their parent's sexual orientation, it is possible to persuade a court that the sexual orientation has no negative impact on the children and therefore should not provide a basis for custodial removal.

However, many children will react negatively and act out with regard to being told that their parent is lesbian or gay. Our children grow up in a homophobic world, their straight parent may have taught them homophobic values, and we ourselves in a closeted period may have reinforced such values. Even if our children personally don't feel rejecting of our homosexuality, they may have justifiable anxieties about how our sexual orientation will be viewed by their peers or the rest of their social world. No matter how lovingly and carefully we communicate the information about our orientation, many of our children take it badly, at least for a while. This is not necessarily fatal in a struggle over custody, however.

A recent Suffolk County Superior Court decision involved a 13-year-old boy who was acting out and feeling negative about his father's being gay. [*M.A.B. v. R.B.*, (NY SupCt Suffolk Cty, 12/2/86) (13 FLR 1136)]. Nonetheless the court granted the father custody. Recognizing that the child would "have genuine social pressure to grapple with and will require strength to integrate the fact of his father's homosexuality into his own life," the court went on to point out that such issues would be true for this boy regardless of which parent had custody, and cited with approval a United States Supreme Court case

194

which refused to allow a custody award to a white father in order to protect a child from the racial prejudice she was expected to confront while living with her white mother whose second husband was black. [*Palmore v. Sidoti*, 466 US 429 (1984)].

The Suffolk County court opinion notes, in justifying its decision that the child's best interests would be served by being in the gay father's custody, that the

> father's behavior has been discreet, not flamboyant. His relationship to his partner is apparently stable and of eight years duration. Testimony was given and not challenged that neither had engaged in any other homosexual relationships. The father acknowledges that [the boy's] sexual orientation is heterosexual and he has stated he has no intention of interfering with this. [13 FLR 1136].

The court was admittedly also choosing between this "discreetly" gay father and a mother who had been experiencing repeated hospitalizations for causes not explained in the opinion. Thus the comparison the court faced was not a simple one of an unquestionably fit straight parent and a gay parent. Nonetheless, the language of this opinion is encouraging in its recognition that a child's need to adjust to the fact of a parent's homosexuality, even when that adjustment involves clear evidence of emotional anxiety and conflict, is not enough to make the parent's homosexuality a proper basis on which to decide custody.

New York falls into the group of states which has had a series of court decisions favorable to gay and lesbian parents. Some of the other states with favorable decisions, at either the trial or appellate level or both, include Alaska, California, Delaware, Massachusetts, New Jersey, Vermont, and Washington. This does not mean that such states have not also had decisions negative to lesbian or gay parents. In many states, trial level decisions are inconsistent with each other and will continue to be so at least until each state's highest court has decided a few appeals in this area.

The laws applicable to decisions about child custody and visitation are open-textured, leaving vast discretion in the hands of the individual trial judge, whose opinions are almost never reported and whose decisions are not bound by other trial-level decisions about other families. These general characteristics of family law often leave gay and lesbian parents at the mercy of individual judges' biases. It is thus crucial for any lesbian or gay parent facing court proceedings about custody or visitation where sexual orientation is going to be raised to prepare a case that will educate the judge in the process of presenting the evidence.

Where possible, having developed ongoing relationships with some experts such as a psychologist or a child development specialist will help. The parent thinking ahead may want to consult with such a person before coming out to children and may want to develop a record of having sought and followed expert advice about how to help children adjust to the information. At the litigation stage, competent legal help is crucial, but attorneys may need to be educated as well as judges. There are many studies available which show that children raised by lesbian mothers are indistinguishable psychologically from children raised by heterosexual mothers. [Hoeffer, "Children's Acquisition of Sex Role Behavior in Lesbian-Mother Families," 51 AM. J. ORTHOPSYCHIATRY 536 (1981); Kirkpatrick, "Lesbian Mother Families," 12 PSYCHIATRIC ANNALS 842 (1982); Kirkpatrick, Smith and Roy, "Lesbian Mothers and Their Children: A Comparative Survey," 51 AM. J. ORTHOPSYCHIATRY 545 (1981); Mandel and Hotvedt, "Lesbians as Parents, A Preliminary Comparison of Heterosexual and Homosexual Mothers and Their Children," *Huisants en wetenschap* (1980); Miller, Jacobsen and Bigner, "The Child's Home Environment for Lesbian and Heterosexual Mothers: A Neglected Area of Research," 7 J. HOMOSEXUALITY 49 (1981); Shavelson, Biaggio, Cross and Lehman, "Lesbian Women's Perceptions of Their Parent-Child Relationships," 5 J. HOMOSEXUALITY 205 (1980).] There are also numerous law review articles that can help legal counsel develop arguments for a court. [*See, for example,* Sheppard, "Lesbian Mothers II: Long Night's Journey Into Day," 8 WOMEN'S RTS. L. RPTR 219 (1985) and the references contained therein; *see also,* Hitchens, "Social Attitudes, Legal Standards and Personal Trauma in Child Custody Cases," 5 J. HOMOSEXUALITY 89 (1979/80).] Much of this information or references to it can be found in the *Lesbian Mother Litigation Manual* and *Lesbian Mothers and Their Children: An Annotated Bibliography of Legal and Psychological Materials*; both are available from the Lesbian Rights Project (1370 Mission St., 4th Floor, San Francisco, CA

94103). The American Civil Liberties Union (132 W. 43rd St., New York, NY 10036) and Lambda Legal Defense and Education Fund (666 Broadway, New York, NY 10012) maintain information about and copies of pleadings from legal cases around the country involving gay and lesbian parents and child custody. The ACLU and the National Lawyers Guild (S.F. Bay Area NLG, 558 Capp St., San Francisco, CA 94110) have publications for lesbian and gay parents.

Being gay or lesbian is legally risky for parents. Coming out to children can sometimes improve the legal odds, by allowing the parent and children to adjust to the issue and to document their ongoing healthy parent-child relations. In other families, coming out can exacerbate the legal situation, because the child reacts negatively or the other parent documents for presentation in court evidence of the child's knowledge and concerns about how that knowledge may have already impacted or will in the future impact the child. Where a parent lives matters in evaluating the risks. But finally, the personal costs of closeting from children, which may mean constraining one's adult life even to the point of celibacy, and the damage such closeting does to one's relationship of trust and love with the child, may outweigh for many parents and children the often illusory legal benefits of keeping secrets. The challenge in the future will be to persuade more and more courts and legislatures that parental sexual orientation, and a child's awareness of it, is not an appropriate basis for denying a good parent custody or visitation.

WHEN THE WALLS BETWEEN PEOPLE CRUMBLE
Melody DeMeritt

My son Zachary is now thirteen years old, sitting on the verge of manhood and not yet wanting to leave boyhood. Soon he will grow up and be an adult making decisions of his own; I'm glad he's getting some practice doing that now. Nearly two years ago I told him that I am a lesbian. I had dreadful expectations about doing this, yet this information has given Zak the opportunity to practice an open-mindedness that will make his future decisions more fair and his contribution to a better world more worthy.

Telling him that I am a lesbian gave him more freedom to make decisions of his own and a realization that he too can stand outside the norms of society, go against the crowd, while being more loving towards himself and others. He understands there are many kinds of people in the world, so he won't be able to focus, as much of the world does, on heterosexual white males as the norm. Zak is more ready to meet the people living in this world who hold different values and come from cultural backgrounds unlike his. I feel he will value all of them because I'm living in a way outside the "norms," and I told him about it.

The fast-changing and multi-cultural world of the future will need open-minded people. If there is any hope for that kind of world, it lies with our children. When I told Zak that I am a lesbian, I broke down old, entrenched notions he had adopted about his world. And since then Zak has made opportunities for himself to knock down the walls around the segments of our society to create "OUR" world, inclusive of all people. Letting him know that I am a lesbian has had none of the dreadful results I expected. Instead, it has led to positive growth in Zak that I had not imagined.

A friend of Zak's came to visit one weekend recently. On Saturday morning after breakfast they got into that rough-and-tumble wrestling that children do as they try to cling so desperately to childhood. They chased back and forth and wrestled, until they were creating quite a ruckus in the house. They ran through the kitchen, feet pounding, when I started to tell them to knock it off and take their "roughhousing" outside. As I turned toward them I saw that Zak had his arm wrapped around his friend's neck from behind in a tight "death hold." I was alarmed, but Zak just looked up at me with a silly look on his face and said with a smile and a wink, "Lovers' quarrel . . ."

At thirteen years of age, I remember being deathly afraid of saying anything with the implications that statement held. As a thirteen-year-old, I had developed an obsessive and heartfelt crush on a good friend of mine. I had no idea what it would mean in the narrow eyes of my social peers to write her love letters, so I did. Well, she cancelled our friendship and shared my notes with everyone else in the junior high school we attended. The kids all then called me homo, queer, fag. I had never heard these words before, nor had I heard the terms lesbian or homosexual. What I clearly understood, though, was that there are certain ways society wants you to behave, and some ways it will not allow. Once I had chosen to go against society, I was ostracized and called names. After that I felt no more love for my friend; I knew only one emotion — fear. I learned fear quite well, and it became my homophobia, locking me in a closet for nearly 20 years.

Thank God it's a different world for Zak. And thank goodness Zak has a "different" mother. Zachary is free of a lot of the fears I had. Certainly some change in our society is responsible for that. Society has moved towards acceptance of people who don't fit the white male heterosexual model through the civil rights movement, the feminist movement, and a growing awareness of the needs and rights of differently abled people. Yet, what has really helped Zachary to be free of the same fears I had as a thirteen-year-old was my telling him that I am a lesbian. He lives with a gay person and loves a gay person. He respects a gay person because she is his mother.

Once he understood that he could love and respect me, he was able to extend that almost immediately to other gay people. The first sign I had that Zak was going to take this news as an opportunity for positive growth came when he talked to his father after learning I am a lesbian. Zachary was living with his father and visiting me on weekends when I told him. As he returned home with his dad Sunday evening, he chose to immediately share the news with his father; yet the way he told his father revealed that he was already changing his attitude and even more remarkably, trying to change the attitude of others. He broke the news by saying, "Well, dad, we can't tell any more gay jokes because we've got a gay person in the family." My ex-husband could not figure who Zak meant, so Zak clarified for him by saying, "Dad, mom is a lesbian."

Zachary had learned almost immediately that you can't create a "we–them" mentality about certain groups of people. He couldn't go on telling jokes about "those people" because one of those people was in his group. The butt of gay jokes which Zachary had heard from his father and probably told to his friends was his mother. He could no longer tell those jokes without hurting me, and the walls of stereotypes between people came crumbling down for him. Zak had also learned that you can safely share information with someone else. In fact, if you try to keep something secret it will later backfire on you. Zak did not want his father to feel excluded from the information, as I had caused Zak to feel.

Since then Zak has broadened his understanding. He realizes that society draws circles around all kinds of groups and says "These are the Hispanics." "These are the poor." "These are the homeless." This society which draws a huge wall around a "majority" of white, male, middle class heterosexuals tries to say that those other circles of people can't fully participate in society because they are different. But those arbitrary structures which society has made evaporated that day for Zak, and there were no longer clear distinctions between groups. All people deserve his love and respect. He learned about my lesbian identity and has used it as a positive source in his life so that he now thinks more open-mindedly about all kinds of people.

Despite the positive effects which I see now, I took a long time coming out to Zak. I had no idea that there could be positive effects of my coming out to anyone, let alone my son. When I first started coming out to people, even the closest of friends and family, I believed there would only be a repeat of my junior high school experience. My friends would never talk to me again and would have reason to be very disappointed with me. Somehow their love would be cut off from me, and I couldn't stand that thought. And the one person whose love I truly needed was my son, so he was one of the last to know. (To this day I regret that I kept him away from his real mother and showed so little trust of his love for me.)

Soon after accepting myself as a lesbian, I began coming out. I came out to an old high school friend, then I came out to my counselor. I came out to my best friends, then I came out to my sisters. I even came out to my father, but I still had not told Zachary.

The friends I told became my support system for figuring out what to do about Zak. I got strange advice like, "It's only good to come out when you are really happy and feeling grounded." Well, most of us, in our first months or maybe years of coming out, usually aren't terribly happy as we ourselves accept our homosexuality. Our emotional lives are frequently tumultuous, yet that piece of advice kept me from telling Zak. I never saw the irony that I couldn't be truly happy with myself as long as I was pretending with Zak, a real Catch-22. Another friend advised, "Once you tell Zak, you can never take it back. Once you say it, you can't say you were just kidding." This advice made sense to me then, but it's ludicrous now. Why would I want to take it back and say I was kidding? Once having said it and gotten it out, why on earth would I want to take it back? Once I had trusted someone enough to be honest, why would I want to return to lying?

All of my coming-out experiences had been very positive. People did more than cope with the information; they congratulated me and encouraged me. Many thanked me for my honesty and said it was good to feel they truly knew me. It had become logical to believe that Zak would react in much the same way, yet I would not tell him. I actively lived as a lesbian for three years before I told him. I was living with my lover when I told Zak. Her children were living with us and they knew. It was so obvious, and everyone but Zak knew. I never thought about that before telling him, yet now it is my only regret.

Over the years I have given myself some informal rules about coming out to people. I have to come out when staying in the closet begins to inhibit conversation. I try to create an occasion specifically for coming out, and I try to do it face to face and at a time when there will be plenty of time to talk about it if needed. But when I finally told Zachary, I broke all of my rules.

It was late one night when we both were very tired, and it was blurted out as an angry reaction to the evening's events. We had attended an open house party thrown by some very old heterosexual friends of mine. As is typical at those events, people were identified as one half of a couple. If someone saw Joe Smith in the kitchen, they would inevitably say "Oh, Mary must be here." When you were introduced, you were assumed to be one half of a couple when people asked, "Who did you come with," or the more cliched "Where's your better half?" People at the party that night were being linked up in pairs, like we were getting ready to step up onto The Ark. I watched this phenomenon of identifying animals in the room — "Oh, we've got a hippo here, there must be another hippo in the room." However, my lover and I were not recognized as a couple; and she was made to feel like an outsider, so she left early. Zak and I stayed for a while longer, but I grew angry about our society and the assumptions it draws about people, so we too left.

As Zak and I drove away for our twenty-minute ride home, I started talking about social rules and how people get married, and "Isn't it funny how it's always Mr. and Mrs. so and so — usually with a man's name." I told Zak I hoped by the time he grew up that women could retain their identities even into marriage. In the midst of all this I dropped the statement, "Zachary, I am a homosexual." By this time, after ten o'clock at night, with me lecturing him for the past fifteen minutes, the boy was half asleep, but he abruptly sat straight up in his seat and seemed awkward and stiff. I asked, "Do you understand what that means? I love Liz in a way that is the kind of love you see between men and women." He only nodded and didn't speak at all. I asked him, "Do you want to talk about this?" By that time we were close to home and he said, "No, I understand. It's okay."

However, the next morning Zachary came to me early and asked, "Mom, could you take a walk with me so we could have a little talk?" I knew he wanted "private time," and I knew what we would talk about.

As we walked, he began by saying, "Well, I have to ask you a question. Are you a homo sapien?" For all the questions I expected, this one threw me completely off guard and I started to laugh. "Zak," I said, "I think you've got the wrong term there. We are all homo sapiens." This broke his stiffness as he began to laugh and said, "Oh mom, I meant are you a homosexual?" At last facing my son as my true self

I said, "Yes, I am a homosexual, and for women we use the term lesbian."

His very first reaction was to check "who else knows." This probably began as a safety check for him, figuring that if no one else knew, then we could be safe with my indiscretion and return to what he sensed as "normal." "Does grandpa know?" "Yes, he knows," I answered. "Does Aunt Cathy know?" As I answered yes the realization grew in me that Zachary was beginning to realize how he had been excluded. My sister Cathy lives two hundred miles away, yet Zak knew that even she had known but he hadn't. "When did you tell grandpa? When did you tell Aunt Cathy?" I knew what his questions were focusing on, and I winced as I had to tell him, "two months ago, two years ago." He asked about my friends, "Do they know?" As I answered "Yes," I knew the underlying message I was giving him: "Everyone has learned this about your mother before you." The lowest point was when he asked if my lover's children knew and I had to answer "yes." The other children in the house had known something so central about his mother and important to his life, but he hadn't known. I could see the hurt on his face, and I could sense the betrayal he felt. Somehow I had managed to leave him out and let everyone else in. I knew immediately that I should have told him sooner, that my son should have been one of the first to know.

What I did to Zachary was unfair. I told all the other important people in my life that I am a lesbian. For Zachary, I hinted. I dropped hints everywhere, depending on a child to figure it out. I guess I hoped that at some subconscious level Zachary already knew, but I never gave him the help and the honesty he needed to understand. Instead I gave clues. Liz and I would hold hands, I would put my arm around her, sit next to her on the couch, sleep in the same bedroom. I had told my friends, talked to them, answered their questions; yet I feared talking to Zachary about it, so I dropped hints instead. I let my fear cause me to treat my son unfairly. I began to fix this the moment I told him and established some honesty between us. I started to fix it when I decided to let him know his mother as she truly is.

I think as parents we would like to shelter our children from harm, from pain, from disappointment. Good parents don't want their children to know that the family's going bankrupt, mommy's lost her job, or there's not enough money to pay the bills.

I grew up the daughter of a woman gravely handicapped since youth with arthritis. I had been exposed to realities that I did not want in my life: my mother's pain and inability to do simple tasks for herself. Perhaps it was this that taught me that my child should be sheltered somehow from having a parent unlike other children's parents. I also had a terrible fear of disappointing or hurting Zachary with the information. By this point in Zachary's childhood I had already managed to accumulate guilt, including the pile of it I acquired when I divorced his father. Perhaps I was acting out of the notion many parents have that as children grow older they will have plenty to cope with, so shelter them when they are young. Yet, in doing so we cause them to miss valuable lessons in coping that will help them to live better adult lives.

If we are lucky, we learn coping skills when we are young which will help us survive the assaults of adolescence and adulthood. Zak had had to cope with his share of stresses as a child. His father and I divorced when he was only four years old; Zak learned how to deal with the temptation to divide loyalties and how to cope with the pain of missing something he badly wanted . . . one family unit. Five years later, when Zak was nine and long before he would know of my lesbianism, he went through depression and guilt to finally decide that he wanted to live with his father 30 miles away. It was very difficult for me to see him go, but I assured him of my love and offered him a permanent open door at my home. Though it was difficult for Zak when he told me the truth of what he wanted, he learned that it is possible to tell someone news they don't want to hear and still have that person love you. If I loved him enough, I would find ways to deal with his decisions about his own life.

This was a lesson that would take me, a mature adult, another two years to learn. It took me that much longer to tell him I'm a lesbian.

The bottom line is that when we give our children the information that we are homosexuals, in addition to possibly causing some temporary pain, we also give them an opportunity to gain valuable insights. Zachary first learned about acceptance, the acceptance of different lifestyles and systems of belief. He was understanding a lesson that took me until age 34 to learn — the lesson of multiculturalism. There are different cultures on this earth and in the United

States, and there needs to be a growing acceptance and valuing of those cultures and of the people who are a part of them.

Zak has surprised me with his ability to benefit himself with the information that I am a lesbian, and he has surprised me with his courage many times. Last year in school he was in a drama class and they were doing impromptu acting. The teacher would create a situation for them and the students would have to make up lines to fit. The situation she gave them one day was that a professor at a university had been murdered. Zak was to act the part of a detective and find out who murdered the professor. His job for the class was to make up the questions a detective would ask the murdered professor's maid, his neighbor, and his friend.

When Zak's turn arrived, he walked on stage and first asked the maid, "How was he murdered?" He had been stabbed in the back. He next asked, "Who had he been dating? Did he have a girlfriend or boyfriend?" At that line, the teacher stopped him. The class was snickering and the teacher interrupted saying, "You mean . . . did he have a girlfriend — don't you?" Zachary answered, "No, I have to ask this because I don't know if he's a homosexual or not. He might be." The teacher acquiesced so Zak went on despite the giggling class. That day Zak went public with his growing awareness that you can't make assumptions about anyone, and you especially can't assume that everyone is a heterosexual. When Zak found out I was a lesbian, all the stereotypical notions of what homosexuals look like were blown away. In his impromptu questioning of the maid, Zak was sharing with the class and his teacher that you can't just assume people are heterosexual. For everyone there is the option that they might be either homosexual or heterosexual.

Zak has met many of our lesbian friends and attended picnics and beach parties with the group. In this, he has not only enlarged the circle of gay people in his life, but he has also learned to value women and feminist ethics. One day we went to a beach barbecue, and at the end of the evening as people were leaving, all of the women stayed to help others carry their belongings to the cars. We formed a spontaneous line of women to hoist heavy ice chests and chairs up a cliff of rocks. Zak pitched in to help and had a lot of fun. As we drove away he said how much he liked my friends and that he had found our beach party different from others he had gone to. At those he had seen women cooking and men carrying. He had seen women cleaning up and individual groups staying to themselves. Yet, with the women he said he had seen more care and equality. "You all hug one another and you sing together," he said, "and it seems like you all protect one another and help out."

This is a quality of lesbian groups, but I told Zak that all people can be just as caring toward each other and struggle for equality in their relationships. "Society tries to tell people how to behave," I said. "Where do you think they got the idea that men empty the trash and women wash the dishes? So, heterosexuals find themselves following all these rules and have a difficult time doing anything else because they think that's normal. But lesbians get a chance to make up new rules for relationships since there are no rules given to them." This was a difficult and abstract lesson for him which I wasn't sure he appreciated, so I went on, "You may not think people can change, but after all, Zak, that's what I had to do when I changed lifestyles." Despite what he got from that discussion, I know that Zak is gaining an understanding about behavior that he might not have had before my "coming out" to him. He is learning a style of living that I hope he will take to his future.

I'm hopeful for Zachary's future. I am hopeful that people will in the next five to ten years realize that homosexuals have a right to their choice of partners. Society's acceptance of us depends on our courage to be proud of who we are and honest about our right to love who we wish. When they know that we truly are everywhere, only then will they become more accepting. At the very least, telling our children, the holders of society's future, will help this acceptance to come about.

One night as I was taking Zak back to his father's house, he began asking about how I could have been married to a man if I was a homosexual. Then he asked, "Mom, if you left your husband and became a lesbian and Liz left her husband and became a lesbian, then how will I know when I marry that my wife won't leave me the same way?" Truly a valid question for a child who had seen lots of children at our lesbian gatherings, who had heard other lesbians talk about "when I was married . . ." My answer may have seemed optimistic, but it showed my honest hope for our future.

"Zachary, some day young people will feel freer to live gay lifestyles if that is what they choose. Society won't harass gay people as much and will give them equal rights. Some day, young people will not have to

212

worry that they will lose their jobs if they are known to be gay. They won't be called names or be put down. When society gets like this young men and women will choose more wisely the lives they lead. Then fewer lesbians and gay men will wind up married to someone of the opposite sex, and fewer will be leaving their husbands and wives." This reassured him that night, but I hope he heard the larger message as well: When we accept each other, we enable honesty and stop the lies and pain.

It has been a slow and gradual process changing society's stereotyping and hatred of the gay community, but the changes come faster and faster as more of us decide to come out and show the world that we are their teachers, their nurses, their lawyers, their mothers and fathers. I have never regretted telling Zachary that I am a lesbian. As soon as I came out to him we grew closer in our relationship, and he grew in his acceptance of all people. All parents hope their children will make the future better; by telling Zachary, I feel I've given him that opportunity.

MAKING THE FANTASY
COME TRUE
Judith Galas

My daughter was in third grade when she told me she thought she was gay. "Mommy," she said, as she stood beside me in our dimly lit Montana basement. "Mommy, I think I'm a homosexual."

I stopped hanging clothes. I remember being curious, but not shocked or annoyed with Amy's news. I think I was bemused by this little girl, so serious and resolved, declaring herself to be something she couldn't possibly understand.

"Why do you think so?" I asked.

She spoke of her playground that afternoon and how she ran up to her teacher and tried to give her a big hug. I pieced together that this teacher had told her girls don't hug each other and she had pulled away from Amy's embrace.

I told Amy I didn't think she was a homosexual, but if someday she again thought she was, it would be okay. I told her not to worry, because gay people lead full and happy lives.

"Some people you know are gay," I told her.

"Really! Who?"

I remember laughing at her curiosity and telling her that they would share their secret with her when they were ready. I don't remember now if I counted myself among the gays who were keeping their secret from her.

Seven years after I'd married, I intellectually discovered lesbianism. The idea that I might love women came clearly to me on a tree-lined, sandy road in Minnesota. I'd just heard Jill Johnston speak at a nearby college. I didn't like her abrupt, disdainful style, the challenge in her voice and manner, but I loved her message — women should love other women.

I couldn't imagine kissing a woman, much less putting my hand or tongue between her legs, but the idea that women were meant to hold and love their own kind appealed to me. The message, though different from anything I'd ever thought, felt right. More than that, it felt liberating.

Sex with my husband felt like bondage. As a virgin on my wedding night, I was disappointed and baffled by sex. I remember my husband as sexually demanding. Easily aroused and constantly focused on

215

sex, he overwhelmed me at first, then frightened and angered me as the years wore on. I never desired his body, but I wanted him — his approval and concern.

I fantasized that without the pressures to perform, to act sexy and always fake interest, I could develop a close friendship with my husband that would satisfy my wish for emotional intimacy.

Somehow seeing a woman as a love object calmed my fears about what I had come to believe was my own sexual dysfunction. More than a husband hater, perhaps I was a lover of women. I decided on that empty road that I would never have sex with my husband again. I didn't want a divorce. I didn't want to hold another woman. I only wanted to be in control of my own body.

It was a shallow promise — broken almost immediately under the strain of my husband's disappointment and pressure. I didn't act on Johnston's message for years, but I never released the hope that lesbianism would free me.

Six years later, having held one woman in my arms, I accepted my gayness. My husband and I spoke the word "lesbian," and inwardly I put on the identity. We were overwhelmed with sadness and loss. As a lesbian I couldn't stay married. I knew our marriage would someday be over, but for all its strain and pain, that relationship encompassed my adult life. I knew nothing else.

I came out to my daughter that year. Her dad and I faced her across the table in a sunny Kansas kitchen. I don't know why we decided it was time to tell her. We had no immediate plans to separate. We kept putting it off with excuses — financial stability, my master's degree, his doctoral work, Amy's age.

216

She was only nine, but somehow she seemed so capable of hearing and understanding. When I told her I was gay, she immediately asked two questions: "Does that mean you don't love Daddy any more?" and "Are you leaving us?" To her, my words meant separation and possibly the end of love.

That moment and my big announcement must have had little impact on Amy — she doesn't remember it. Now 19, Amy has reserved a different coming out memory — one I barely remember. For a college theme assignment dealing with homosexuality, she wrote

> I was sitting in my parents' room on their big bed. Actually, I was sitting in my mother's room on her bed. My parents had just gotten a divorce. I was watching her in the mirror as she brushed her hair. I asked her why she looked so happy, and she told me she had fallen in love. I asked with whom, and she said, "Jill."

She goes on to say

> It took me a long time to think about things and to sort out my feelings. It finally came down to this — I loved my mother. To reject homosexuality was to reject her — I couldn't.

Like other gays, I've been afraid of being rejected by someone, at some time. Gays live with the fear and sometimes the rejection. But rejection by our children is another matter. An emotional Richter

Scale to measure the impact of child rejection on a gay parent would have to read Magnitude 8 — capable of tremendous damage. Yet, in spite of the fear, many parents do tell their children.

I've seen gay-parent-and-child relationships not only survive this honesty, but also blossom in a new stage of truth and sharing. But I've also heard women tearfully speak of their children's rejection. The trust and rapport the parents and children shared before the announcement seems to be critical to whether the parent will hear "I still love you" or "You're a pervert."

When I met Ann and Nancy, they were 10 years into a love affair. One was still married and living with her husband. The other had divorced about four years earlier. Each had three children who were either in college or almost there. Ann's ex-husband knew she was gay, but Nancy's husband did not, nor did any of their children.

During that decade, their attempts to get together as they juggled two husbands and six children must have resembled the staging of a Moss Hart comedy — false exits, secret meetings, innuendo, subtlety and organization. Most of the time when they spoke of those years, they weren't laughing. They said they coped and the lies drained them.

One evening, about five years into her relationship with Nancy, Ann's children saw a TV movie about two women who had fallen in love with each other. Ann's young teenage son came into the kitchen and announced, "Those women act like you and Nancy." Ann remembers joking about the absurdity of his statement. "Nancy and I are just very good friends," she explained. But she recalls being stunned by his accurate observations.

When Ann's son was about 20, he discovered a loving birthday message from Nancy to his mother. He asked his mother about the card. Again she spoke of her special friendship with Nancy, their closeness, but she denied anything else. By this time, Ann wanted to tell her children, but the well-developed lie made it difficult.

She decided her son's question had showed far more courage than her answer. Later that night she came out to him. His support and warmth encouraged her to tell her two daughters when the time was right. When her and Nancy's relationship floundered, Ann's children were able to do what families are supposed to do during hard times — they hugged, encouraged, listened and loved. Ann's openness gave her children the chance to see her as a person who struggled and grieved.

Ann adores her kids. Watching her with her daughters, it's easy to see the joy, warmth and caring that connects them. Extremely proud of her children, Ann cheers them, helps them, and in every way shows them they are central to her life. They adore her in return. Her lesbianism hasn't eroded those feelings.

Another friend of mine, however, showed me the painful side of coming out. Barbara's children attacked her when they discovered her hidden life. When I met Barbara, she was a divorced college professor with two teenage daughters and a nine-year-old son. Her oldest daughter chose to live nearby with her father. Barbara believed their relationship was strained because her daughter suspected Barbara was a lesbian. Barbara said she thought her daughter also might be a lesbian and ambivalence about her own sexuality made her fear her mom.

Letters from Barbara over the next few years told the story of a woman who eventually lost custody of all three children. Her children, she said, had rejected her. She hoped time would bring understanding and reconciliation.

Even before those letters, when we still talked about feminism, lesbianism and motherhood over glasses of wine, I realized Barbara was an alcoholic. She sadly admitted that while drunk she had hit her oldest daughter hard across the face. Her children accused her of embarrassing them and of never being able to control her mouth when she was drinking.

Barbara's children must have been angry when they saw her stumble around. Her words and sometimes her hands hurt them. I think they blamed their mother for the divorce and in their anger and confusion they turned on her. Once they knew she was gay, they chose the easiest and most hurtful weapon they had — "I hate you, you queer."

I had encouraged Barbara to come out to her children. I believed if she was honest, she could help them understand her new life. I thought honesty would make Barbara feel less guarded when she was with them. When Barbara's children turned on her, I was reminded that angry, hurt children can be very cruel. They may use whatever they can to get even with their parents, and their words can sting.

When Barbara's children turned on her, their rejection taught me something. I learned that a parent/child relationship already under siege when the parent comes out may be damaged even further if the children use gayness as fresh fuel in the ongoing battle.

Amy and I, unlike Barbara and her children, were not embroiled in any battles when I came out. Still, in spite of the calm, I braced for future confrontations. I assumed that most children, even the usually cooperative ones, will do or think the exact opposite of what their parents wish. Many of the teenagers I saw seemed to go through a phase of rejecting parental values.

Even Amy's dad, an atheist who vilifies Miss America, lived in fear that Amy would become a beauty queen before entering the convent. She hasn't — yet.

In spite of my fears, Amy hasn't rejected my values and lifestyle. I thought I would hear things like, "You embarrass me," or "Don't come to my play with Cindy," or "Don't tell people you're gay." To my surprise I didn't.

Most of the out mothers I know seemed to experience a similar acceptance from their children. Oh, I remember one teenager stomping to another section of the basketball bleachers because her mother and her friends were "acting like a bunch of dykes." But none of the mothers who had been out to their children from the beginning ever spoke of any grand rejection.

It's a family joke that Amy's come out for me more than I've come out for myself. At first she selectively told her friends about her mom, particularly those she thought might come to the house. As she grew older, she was less selective. Now

I think all her friends know. In fact, in some odd way having a gay mother appears to be chic.

But while having a gay mom may be chic, being gay yourself probably is not. Most of the daughters of the lesbians I know are presently straight. As a young teenager Amy thought she should break her straightness to me gently. "Mom, I don't think I'm gay," she told me. When she delivered her "I'm straight" message, she already had close friendships with other gay teenagers and was beginning to think about boys. I think my lesbianism gave her a sense of option and tolerance of choice.

We have never quarrelled over my lifestyle, and she is fond of my lover Cindy. A warm step-parent/step-child relationship has grown between them. But while she verbally supports my lifestyle and is comfortable with my mate, I don't think she sees my life as normal. She doesn't live in a society that tells her it's okay to be gay.

For almost a year, Amy has had a male lover — her first. Amy says she suspects her grandmother is totally silent about her intimate relationship with this young man not because she approves, but because she is relieved. "Maybe grandma doesn't say anything because she's thinking, 'at least she's normal,'" Amy offers with a laugh.

She may be right. My mom calls Cindy her "third daughter," but I suspect she would be delighted if I told her I had fallen in love with a man and that my lesbianism was a phase I had passed through.

Unwittingly, I've heard my mother, my daughter, and the children of other lesbians call straights normal. "They're not gay," my mother once said about some young men she knew. "They're normal."

Amy and she laughed, and then my mother corrected herself and said, "You know what I mean." Yes, I did.

No matter what we may want the world to think about gay men and lesbians, the world is not likely to call us "normal" — not in our lifetime. My daughter accepts my gayness. As she gains more experience, I hope she also comes to see it as normal.

I don't think my lesbianism pushed her into a relationship with a man, but I suspect she felt some relief when she was attracted to one. She admits to wanting and needing a boyfriend, even while she struggles with not wanting the one she has.

She seems to measure her own maturation only against my heterosexual history. At 16, I met her father. When she was 16, she said, "It's scary to think that any day now I might meet my husband." She knows I was engaged when I was not quite 19 and married a year later. She says with assertion, "I don't want to marry."

She has my example of being a lesbian after a straight marriage and a child, but that example doesn't seem to trigger her sense of sexual choice and possibility. She hasn't said she will never love a woman, but she also has never said someday she might.

In a world that sees gayness as abnormal, Amy sees herself as straight. I think the social taboo against homosexuality is too strong for her yet to even consider the possibility that someday she might love a woman.

I assume that one day I will have a son-in-law. I also assume, however, that I might have a "daughter-in-law." My own mother watched me make a commitment with a woman after 14 years of marriage to a man.

My relationship with that man is now distant and chilly. But we never bad-mouth each other to Amy. She says she is grateful we never forced her to take sides. I sometimes wonder what she has pieced together about my married years.

Amy says she remembers my depression and my withdrawal when I was married, but I don't think she can pick out the causes. She is still too inexperienced to relate her feelings and struggles in relationships to the power struggles I was facing with her dad.

She has no trouble saying that my joy, zest, spontaneity and peace came with my lesbianism. To Amy, I am prettier, happier and more successful now than when I was married. But she has difficulty saying the marriage was unhappy or that her dad was a frightening, often demanding man then.

I think my lesbianism and my feminism have made Amy defensive for men in general and protective of her father in particular. While I never speak negatively of men as a class, my life proves I don't need a man — the ultimate insult.

She shared a story with me once about how her dad's male friends closely interviewed his new girlfriend. They wanted to be sure another woman wouldn't break his heart. Those men believed I victimized her dad.

I don't know if Amy agrees with them. She probably is unclear herself. It seems difficult for Amy to see that her dad's and my unhappy marriage grew from many issues — a lack of trust, respect and honesty — not just sexual preference. It is the sexual part that seems most obvious to her. Sex, she has said, is why her parents divorced.

Relationships, my daughter is learning, are complex and sometimes difficult. She has little experience to help her understand the issues I struggled with as a wife — identity, dignity, my place in the world, my connection to others and myself. She hasn't resolved those issues for herself. For now, it might be easier for her simply to blame sex for my marriage's end.

Many non-gays also believe homosexuality simply is a matter of sex. Because they are focused on the sex in the gay relationship, they believe gays set bad examples for children. I have known gay parents who wonder if their gayness might harm their children's sexual development or distort their sense of what is wholesome and good.

Often when I look back on my marriage, I worry about whether my "normal" marriage distorted Amy's ideas of what makes a wholesome relationship. I remember my marriage as a time of sad compliance — sexually and emotionally. Did I unintentionally teach her that women must be compliant?

Inwardly I was beaten, unable to take control of my body or my life. I thought of relationships as something you always struggled with. Those years were mostly joyless, but I believed I should be responsible and hold on. I waited patiently for that one hour, that day or week when everything connected between me and my husband, when our laughter came easily and our closeness was real. Did my patience teach Amy that women must simply endure, even when there was no you?

Rather than worry about what gay relationships teach their children, gay parents must remember that their homosexual unions can give their children healthy examples of commitment, nurture and love. Four years ago Cindy and I chose each other as life companions. Together we give Amy a much better example of a respectful, loving relationship than I ever did when I lived with her father.

Cindy and I help each other, whether we're struggling through the housework or collapsing after a particularly hard day. Amy has few if any memories of her father helping me, whether it was with housework or child care or simply with a supportive embrace. Examples of nurture and care abound in Cindy's and my home, and when Amy visits I know she feels the warmth we share.

"Why don't you and Cindy get tired of each other?" she asked me the other day.

I knew she was measuring the elasticity in my relationship against the more rigid and increasingly difficult bond she shared with her boyfriend.

Being open with Amy about my lesbianism has given me another chance to show her how healthy relationships work. I also believe my openness encourages her to be open about her life. Because I've discussed the taboo of lesbianism with her, perhaps she has felt more comfortable discussing her taboos of premarital sex and birth control with me.

How many parents worry when their children withdraw into silence? Young people often won't talk about their troubles, hurts and fears, but as parents we still sense them. There have been times when I've wanted to shake Amy and force her to reveal herself, peel back her defenses and show me the young woman inside. As her parent, I want to be a part of her life and I am so pleased when her sharing makes it possible for me to know her better. She, in turn, seems pleased that I have trusted her with my lesbianism and secrets about my life.

I believe our children will try to be as honest with us as we try to be with them. If we leave out a major chunk of our lives — our gayness — our children will know they are being deceived. Oh, they may not specifically know the word "homosexual," or the name of our lover, or visualize our actions, but they will know they are being lied to through silence.

I've watched several friends and acquaintances battle with keeping this secret from their children. They lie directly or by omission. Their lovers are called "close friends" or "roommates." If they live with their lovers, they maintain separate bedrooms. Like sinners they scurry in the dark from one bed to another when they think the children are sleeping. Not only are they creating a lie of silence with their children, they are depriving themselves of peaceful, natural relationships with their lovers.

I suspect the earlier a child hears her parent is gay, the easier it is for her to accept that information. Amy learned of my gayness before she was an insecure adolescent. My gayness hasn't seemed to matter any more than my religious or political preferences.

The longer the parent holds on to the lie, the more difficult it may become to end it. Coming out may seem impossible. When we agree to a lie of silence on difficult issues with our children, we

227

guarantee we will only have superficial things to say to each other. I can be superficial with strangers, but not with my child.

I couldn't have lived the life a friend of mine chose. She lived in the same house with her lover and two sons for 10 years. Everyone had separate bedrooms. Kate and Martha obviously were a couple. The four of them were a family, but the women agreed to total silence about Martha's role in Kate's life.

The boys became men and moved away. Kate insists they never knew she and Martha were lovers because the subject never came up. It may never have. But I'd bet a fortune, if I had one, that Kate's boys know their mother is a lesbian. They also know they may never talk about it.

When Martha left, Kate was devastated, but she had no family member to grieve with. Her lie isolated her from the most significant people in her life, her children.

Ironically, Kate thinks one of her sons might be gay — she's not sure. The boys grew up with her firmly enforced rule — gay not spoken here. That silence probably has isolated Kate from her son, even though they now may have a great deal to share.

My gayness aside, parenting has been hard on me. Any parent knows that raising children takes work, sacrifice and time. What I hope I'll receive for those tough years is my daughter's life-long friendship.

I want Amy to be a close friend, someone who respects and admires me, someone whom I can respect and admire. That long-term goal — my daughter's enduring friendship — kept me many times from yelling when I needed to listen, being sarcastic when I needed to be patient, being unyielding when I needed to compromise. It also kept me from lying. I trusted that if I was honest with that little girl, she would be honest with me, and from that honesty would come an adult bond that would nourish us both.

I've read often Adrienne Rich's essay "Women and Honor: Some Notes on Lying." I accept Rich's premise that lying erodes not only our outside reality, but our inner strength. Written for women, I think her words hold a message for any parent who struggles with whether to come out to his or her child. It encourages me to believe that honesty, although difficult, gives people a future with each other.

It isn't that to have an honorable relationship with you, I have to understand everything, or tell you everything at once, or that I can know, beforehand, everything I need to tell you.

It means that most of the time I am eager, longing for the possibility of telling you. That these possibilities may seem frightening, but not destructive, to me. That I feel strong enough to hear your tentative and groping words. That we both know we are trying, all the time, to extend the possibilities of truth between us.

The possibility of life between us.[1]

Sometimes children may seek the truth before their parents feel ready to reveal it. "Are you gay?" a child may ask. Unprepared for the question, the parent's first protective response might be a quick "No." But children deserve the truth.

A child old enough to ask probably is old enough to have wrestled with the discomfort of facing the truth. The fear the parent feels with the question is similar to the fear the child already has worked to conquer. She may have spent days rehearsing the question and building up her courage. Her need to know overpowered her fear. If you lie to her, you negate not only your bravery to face the taboo, but hers.

"If homosexuality were not considered such a distasteful and taboo topic, people would be better able to come to terms with the idea," my daughter said in her college essay. "Most important," she wrote,

> people must realize that homosexuals are not freaks and weirdos or society's fringe elements. They are our mothers, sisters, friends, nephews, teachers, and fathers. . . .
> My mother's fantasy is that, at some agreed-upon time, every gay person in America will stand up and say that he or she is gay. . . . Chances are we will know someone who is standing and chances are we have loved

[1]Adrienne Rich, "Women and Honor: Some Notes on Lying," in *On Lies, Secrets, and Silence, Selected Prose 1966–1978* (New York: W. W. Norton & Company, 1979), pp. 193–194.

them. Knowledge breaks down prejudice. Until we realize how many gay people we really know, we will never lose our fear of deviancy and we will never be able to live respectfully with millions of people.

Amy's right about my fantasy. I do wish all gays could feel safe enough to stand in unison and show everyone we are the people they already love and respect. But while a simultaneous coming out to millions is not possible, private comings out to our children are. I believe that honesty has cemented the relationship I share with my daughter and that this honesty makes life between us possible.

COMING OUT:
THE POLITICS
Delia Cunningham

Having a choice about coming out gives gay and lesbian parents an immense privilege. One's race is an identity that cannot be hidden. One's economic status and the resulting class of society in which one lives becomes obvious in the clothes one wears, the vehicles one drives, the neighborhood where one lives. Sexual preference resulting in an alternative lifestyle, however, creates the privilege of choice. We can dress in role-appropriate drag, play the acceptable social

232

games and hibernate from the rest of society as much as possible. We can even attempt to hide the core of our identity from our family and friends.

Children, however, are not sold on society's appraisal. Like our own parents and lifelong friends, if they care to pay attention to our behaviors, emotions and growth patterns, they will know their parents' true sexual orientation. Just as they will one day discover the truth about Santa Claus or the tooth fairy, they will intuitively realize there is something different about the adults they know and love.

Knowing this gives gay and lesbian parents a new kind of responsibility when it comes to child rearing. There are new questions to be answered, new issues to be considered:

- First, what message are we giving our children and what are we teaching them by our own attitudes toward ourselves and all alternative lifestyles? Second, how are we affecting our future and the future of the planet by what our children learn through our attitudes?
- Then, taking politics outside of the home, what of the attitudes of straight society toward our family? How does the gay and lesbian community make our family feel, and what future is there for us among our own?
- Finally, where is our space? What opportunities are there for creating an alternative family community, a non-exclusive, loving environment where our children can experience the beginnings of our hope for the future?

In the beginning, many gay and lesbian parents attempt to avoid dealing with their lifestyle all together. The throes of divorce can be devastating. The threat of a heterosexual parent using youngsters for power or simply fighting his or her own desperate custody battle is real. It is a time when coming out can mean total loss. Even the most militant parent can understand that a close personal relationship with one's children through troubled times and during the parent's own coming out process cannot be sacrificed willingly.

Of course, a heterosexual parent often saves us the bother of coming out to our children by announcing the fact when we are absent. There is such a thing as coming out in self-defense, because it is improbable that a warring ex-spouse will teach the children about their gay or lesbian parent in a positive, honest manner.

This is also the time when many divorcing parents give up. It seems easier to allow that crack in the parenting relationship to widen for a time, giving us the opportunity to come out properly, to accept ourselves while withdrawing from responsibility. We fail to realize that the damage created by such a breach, when avoidable, may not be worth the toll it takes while we are struggling with self-acceptance and the nuts and bolts of how to come out to our children.

In addition, so-called "protection" of the child's supposed innocence takes on unrealistic dimensions when there is no concrete reason a young person should *not* be exposed to gay culture, both positive and negative. While no one endorses involving children in the bar scene, there are other lesbian and gay groups, social circles and even religious organizations that would offer wide-eyed little ones a very positive image of who their mom or dad really may be and what her or his lifestyle is about.

Parenting offers many, many unreachable goals. We see on television, learn from experts about perfection in child rearing. In return, we hear from psychologists how our parents, particularly our mothers, shaped our lives for better or worse. What a responsibility! It would be overwhelming to embrace fully this perspective of the challenge of parenting when we ourselves are changing daily.

The true question is whether parents can hide their own personal development from their children yet still expect the youngsters to believe in truth, honesty and equality. The lessons we teach our young people are better communicated by opening up to them than by shutting them off to fend for themselves among other (read: straight) people's values.

There is a limit to how long a person can live a lie. When that person is a parent, sometimes residing with a same-sex partner under the same roof as the children, it is unrealistic to expect the children not to see the love and passion between the two adult lovers any more than they would be unaware of the personal exchange between a parent and a step-parent. And why should we hide such a positive emotion as love between equals? Perhaps it is time children of the world are invited to experience a relationship that is by nature closer to equality than any other.

A few authors have addressed primarily heterosexual parents with guidelines on how to raise non-sexist children. These inevitably stress the importance of sharing chores equally, with mother and dad both washing dishes or mowing the lawn or fixing the car. Only when the children see both men and women sharing in all household functions regardless of gender or expected roles will youngsters acknowledge all their choices in life, whether it be in career, marriage or spiritual growth.

There is no reason these rules should change for homosexual parents. In fact, the main difference is a positive one. In a home where *all* adults take shared responsibility without the existence of gender-based roles, children are presented with myriad options for their future. It may be the best possible way to show them how exciting their future could be. There is no reason to dampen this excellent environment with lies, closeted emotions, and other attempts to confuse the child's perceptions.

There is growing national interest in procreation among gay men and lesbians. In one metropolitan area in Florida there are at least a half dozen adoptive parents, and another half dozen biological parents who chose to birth children into gay and/or lesbian households. These offspring may be the most fortunate of all. Their parents have already accepted their lifestyles and are welcoming a new definition of parenting in a new family dimension.

This may be the strongest statement of the gay and lesbian movement, and of the feminist movement. By choosing to create alternative families, by believing in our lifestyles and our futures, we are refusing to deny our need to have loving, whole families. We are creating our own definition, naming ourselves. It is not simply a personal choice, nor is it any rejection of social responsibility. Instead, the choice to become an alternative family is a political statement of a belief in our future and the future of the world. It is a legacy of choice we are giving our children, our planet and ourselves.

The decision to create our own family structure on the fringes of this patriarchal, sexist society is brave. Many do not wish to risk it, and there is no validity in condemning the child-free any more than we should make choices that are not right for us. How much better the state of society would be if those who preferred not to take on the responsibility of parenthood could *always* make that decision with freedom and facts behind them.

At the same time, children born into gay and lesbian families have tremendous opportunity, so long as their parents are comfortable with themselves and are encouraging this open, honest and loving environment within their own homes. At the least, such youngsters learn early about making choices and living true to one's self. At the best, these little ones have the opportunity to discover themselves among an open-minded, supportive community where options in life are the norm and freedom the goal. Coming out is no longer an issue, but part of the process of life.

However, while there is some acceptance of the decision to have and raise children, there is little real support for gay and lesbian families who wish to integrate into our own community. If anything stifles the coming out process and discourages honesty, it is this lack of acceptance of gay and lesbian families within this formerly supportive network. This shows up in a number of ways.

- Lack of child care arrangements or children's alternatives at adult events, social or political.
- Tasteless humor in athletic, social and other events that would otherwise be positive community gatherings where children could be integrated without hassle.
- Failure of other gay and/or lesbian families to make themselves visible within our community, thereby furthering the belief there is no need for family outreach and encouraging parents to keep their life with their children separate from their social life.
- Alienation and isolation of formerly straight gay men and particularly lesbians with children, forcing them to see no alternative to giving child custody to a former spouse. The choice becomes no choice: these parents can live true to themselves in a gay lifestyle or remain isolated most of the time as a single parent until the children are grown.

A lack of *active* acceptance of our alternative families gives parents questioning their sexual preference even more pressure to conform to society's heterosexual expectations.

These issues are not limited to any one segment. They apply to gay groups primarily comprised of male members as well as to women's events. They occur in religious, political, social and other activities. In all cases, the lack of recognition of our children and their place in all of our lives (whether we are biological or custodial parents, or child-free) hurts us all.

Family care (including family and medical leave, child care and long term care), pay equity, housing and public health care are just a handful of the emerging family policy issues confronting Americans today. Concern about family issues is a topic currently being brought to the forefront by national figures such as Congresswoman Pat Schroeder and pediatrician and recognized child-rearing authority Dr. T. Berry Brazelton. Working with them are other people with different kinds of social and political influence such as the creator and producer of *Family Ties*, Gary David Goldberg, and Dr. Diana Meehan, former director of the University of Southern California's Institute for the Study of Women and Men in Society. Currently these leaders are speaking to alternative families with more willingness than are the gay and lesbian community or the feminist community. They do not falter when asked about their definition of family, and they begin their presentation clearly speaking to more than the traditional nuclear unit.

But a few aware leaders cannot be depended on to speak for us — whether our gay and lesbian families involve children, aging parents, or simply supportive bonds between ex-lovers, current lovers and friends. We must begin to define ourselves as families, a factor long missing from gay and lesbian politics. We must come out as families and as parents. We must acknowledge ourselves. If gay men and lesbians do not stand together on this issue, we may always stand alone.

The onset of AIDS and other health concerns encourages the current attitude toward responsibility with personal involvement and longer term commitments. At the same time, there have always been gay and lesbian couples (or other alternative living arrangements) that have endured the test of time. Like gay men and lesbians with children, in the past these stable family units have tended to withdraw from their (and our) own community. Whether they have done so in defense of their bonds, from fear of exposure, or from a lack of desire to socialize, they have also been alienated. A place without networking, without mutual support, is a place of danger.

Take the case of one recently divorced mother of two. After having a lesbian affair for more than a year, this woman began to face the reality of her situation. Strong religious beliefs pulled her to stay married, to deny herself for her children and her husband. But she was coming out. She needed our community's support. When she and her woman lover were together, they spent most of their time alone. It was months before they dared venture to their first gay bar or all-female gathering. The married woman was confused, yet afraid; both women were professionals dealing with children, so their careers were at stake as well. For many months she alternated between denying her lesbian self through religious conviction and dedication to her children, and irresistibly returning to her woman lover where she ached for her offspring and her traditional family support. Finally her husband would accept her return no more. She declined fighting for custody when he threatened to expose her and her lover, having learned about her lesbianism from her own lips when on one return trip to her marriage she felt compelled to confess.

The good news is that she did find personal support in the Metropolitan Community Church. She does see her children frequently, but at those times she is usually forced to withdraw from the gay community and find conventional activities for their family. The gay church currently has no Sunday School, no space for children. Area lesbian groups offer no child care and purposely exclude her son even at his young age. Her life has become the typical dichotomy of the lesbian mother.

Where were we when she needed us? Is the gay community so afraid of repercussion from straight society that we refuse to shelter our own — especially those who may someday be our own? These are not personal questions. This is not personal rejection. This is political — and personal — reality.

If there is a positive aspect here, it is that at least this mother is honest with her children. She has come out, and she has come out to them as is appropriate for their ages. There is no turning back, and no need to return.

But what of her children? What of the children born into a gay and lesbian family? If they are rejected by our community, whether in gender-segregated child care, mindless babysitting arrangements, or total exclusion and lack of acknowledgment, what sort of a world will they

241

present to us when we are ready to retire and grow old? Why should they then support those who rejected them — openly or by the sin of omission?

It is vital that gay and lesbian families (with or without children) join in this political awareness of family issues. For those willing and able to speak out openly, for those able to come out publicly, there is definite need to participate in the movement to make family issues foremost in this country and in the world. However, within the gay and lesbian community there is ample room for those of us aware of the inequities of social structure to speak out and activate change.

The alternatives are bleak. A community that fails to embrace its own is not a community at all, but an elite privileged class. There may be many reasons for child-free gay men and lesbians to take such an attitude — fear of children, ignorance of the closeted parenting among lesbian sisters and gay brothers, rejection of traditional values, and an unwillingness to confront their own decision not to bear and raise children. There is nothing wrong with deciding not to parent. If more people were true to themselves in this respect, perhaps there would be no population explosion, no baby boom. But there must be an acceptance of the place the children who are here play in all of our futures and in all of our todays. After all, ageism is inevitable in any community devoid of children.

How can a community that speaks to the hearing impaired, the handicapped, the chem free, fail to speak to its children? Parents and child-free individuals alike must recognize this need. We must come out as parents, and come out as a community that speaks to the needs of *all* its members, regardless of age. Indeed, children of gay men and lesbians are already a part of our community, whether publicly acknowledged or not.

After all, children can be delightful. How much more wonderful a trip to the beach can be when a youngster is along to point out the excitement of shells. How much more awareness a person can have when a little one holds a grown-up's hand and leads an adventure around a state park.

By discovering our community's children, we will discover ourselves. By recognizing and coming out to ourselves as families, not as isolated adults, we will find a place of leadership in the family movement of today and will reap the benefit of feminist and humanist social change.

We cannot forget that our children are our tomorrows. If we do, they will remind us when we least expect it. If we work together for the betterment of all of us, that reminder will be as filled with joy as they can make our lives today.

AFTERWORD
Loralee MacPike

I have been very fortunate: I didn't have to worry about how to come out to my daughter, and the results have been more positive and enriching than I could have imagined.

I had come out to myself only five months before that August day when Gwynn wrote me her letter. And like many "born-again Lesbians," I was overjoyed at my new-found self and my newly-defined life. Neither my partner nor I had ever been in a Lesbian relationship before, so neither brought to our lives the social foundations and friendships that are part of gay communities; but we began making subtle

244

approaches to others who in one way or another appeared to be coming out to us, and we in turn came out to others — my cousin and my sister, her parents, carefully selected colleagues.

I don't know why, during this time, I never thought about how I would come out to my daughter. Most of the people I came out to were people whose daily lives intersected with mine, and perhaps because my daughter lived with her father 3,000 miles away, I didn't associate "coming out" and "daughter." Thus freed of the worries of how and when to tell, perhaps I was also freed from the fears of what might happen. She told me she knew; and we were still friends, embarked on a wonderful shared vacation that remains one of the high points of our family memories.

But I was lucky. I hadn't been a Lesbian long enough for her to fear I was withholding secrets from her. Our relationship had always been characterized by honesty — about the divorce, about my decision to move away and hers to stay in her home town, with her father — so there was an expectation (on both sides) that we would continue to be honest. From an early age, she considered herself "different'" from her peers in a whole range of ways, so she had learned not only to accept but also to value difference. And her experience with me was that I loved *her*, not her characteristics, so when she accepted my "difference" she was simply following the model she had observed.

As you have seen, not all gay and Lesbian parents and their children tread the same smooth path I did. But despite a multiplicity of difficulties and dangers, all of them have experienced positive results from coming out, even if it be only a personal strengthening of will to work actively against our culture's ingrained homophobia.

To the women and men who have given us their stories in this volume, I extend my sincere thanks for their efforts. The courage, inventiveness, fidelity, and love of these parents shine through all the stories. They show us that risks can be taken and dangers overcome. Most of all, though, they show us that by living the truths of our lives, we can begin to change the world. Every time we come out — to our children or to others — we alter the balance of homophobia in American culture. The truths we can show may be only partial, and they may be communicated to only a few; we are all confined by some circumstances which we cannot defy because the risks are too great. But every tiny piece of the truth about Lesbian and gay people adds to the visibility and reality of Lesbian and gay lives. In this way, every story you have read has dispelled a little bit of homophobia and thus made life better and easier for all of us.

And as we all live the truths that are ours to proclaim, we change — we change ourselves, change our children . . . change the world. The courage and action of the men and women who tell these stories is a step toward the liberation of us all.

CONTRIBUTORS

A. W. I am writing anonymously due to the requests of the children involved. They agreed to the writing and publishing of this piece if all names were changed so that they could not be identified.

We all live what, to us, seems a normal life not unlike anybody else's. In fact, it's easier than many lives: we are not poor, we do not deal with alcohol or drug problems, there is no physical or emotional abuse.

Elliott A. Brager is a lawyer and gay rights activist in Maryland. He is known to his entire community as a fund-raiser par excellence and has been a strong liaison between the gay and straight community.

Stephen Brammeier is a white, middle-class, upwardly mobile veterinarian who shares joint custody of his two sons with his ex-wife.

Jeri Broxterman is a 32-year-old lesbian mother of three, divorced and living with her lover of five years. Her children do not live with her, not of her own choosing but rather that of a judge who understands nothing of her lifestyle. In 1986, she fell prey to a homophobic judicial system and was sentenced to prison for a crime she did not commit. During her incarceration she began writing, and has published stories, poetry and articles across the U.S. and Canada and Sweden. Since her release she has continued to fight for her children and is presently writing a book about her experiences.

Miriam Carroll is a 58-year-old Jewish lesbian activist and writer who earns her living from massage. In 1983 she moved from New Hampshire to Atlanta, GA to start a new life. In Atlanta she has founded a Lesbian Support Group and was a steering committee member for the Southeast Lesbian and Gay Conference (April 1988) and a co-chair of WomanWrites '87, a writers' conference. Remembering her own loneliness and isolation when she moved to Atlanta, she lists her phone number in various publications and outlets so she can be a contact person for newcomers and those needing to find out about local Lesbian activities.

Cathy was born and raised on a ranch in a small East Texas town. Currently she is employed in Austin, Texas, by a major hotel chain in their central reservations office. She is nearing completion of her Elementary Education degree. Bring a single parent as well as a student takes up plenty of time, but she does find some time to pursue outside interests. She is involved in women's soccer, as a coach for her three-year-old daughter's soccer team. Coaching the girls has been challenging, but the rewards far outweigh the challenges. She is also involved as a lobbyist and advocate for government- and employer-funded child care.

B. Victoria Cossette is a 50-year-old crone living in Tampa, Florida with her significant other, two daughters, and several pets. She recently changed her name from Barbara Nesset to B. Victoria Cossette. She is a Lesbian S/M Feminist, mother, counselor, writer, healer, and witch. She is active in the gay community and enjoys her family, home, writing, and reading. She spent 38 years in Minnesota and three years in California before migrating to Florida in 1980. She is enjoying her spiritual growth and studying Wicca.

Delia Cunningham and her partner of eleven years are the mothers-by-choice of three children. A freelance journalist, Delia regularly writes about business topics and women's and family issues. Her current projects include her first novel, *For the Love* *of an Amazon,* and a non-fiction book about her parenting experience, *Double Mothers: The Creative Conception of the Lesbian Family.* Delia and her partner offer workshops on Motherhood by Choice, The Politics of Acknowledging Our Gay and Lesbian Families, and other topics. They participate as a family in gay and Lesbian community activities when possible and are active in the Unitarian Universalist Church.

Joesphine d'Antonio, mother of Joe, 21, Gina, 20, and Peter, 18, lives with Tesa in Audubon, NJ. At the age of five, she had polio and suffered for years from the early "treatments" for that disease. She ran her own school-transportation/limo business for five years and now works as a patient liaison person with AIDS patients in a Philadelphia hospital, helping them feel less alone.

Melody DeMeritt lives in a small college town with her lover of four years and her two teenaged children. Her son, Zachary, moved in during the course of this writing, returning after four years of living with his father. Three teenagers and two working mothers makes for a busy household! Melody has taught English for over ten years at the local college, specializing in composition and business writing. She has also served as a fundraiser and magazine editor and has worked with the local women's resource center press.

Marcia Diane is a social worker for child protective services. She resides in Sonoma County, California. This story is her first published work. She carries the dream of writing Lesbian fiction for fun.

Lynne D'Orsay is a 36-year-old Lesbian making her home with her 6-year-old daughter Hannah, her lover and partner Lisa, and several other Lesbian women in a small New England seaport city. Of primary importance in her life is speaking to — in her own way — the issues and difficulties and joys that arise in our lives as women and Lesbians in this culture. Her other interests involve a seemingly endless fascination with the analysis of her own and others' familial relationships, and an unrelated love of returning the products of our mother earth back to her soil. One of the moments she most prizes is the time her daughter told her kindergarten teacher that "my mommy is a Lesbian, an amazon and a dyke."

Martha Ficklen grew up in coastal North Carolina and raised her sons in coastal Virginia. She has lived in St. Louis for 12 years with her lover, Nan. They are both teachers. Their house is supervised by a blue-eyed cat named Finnegan. Under the name of Carla Flanagan, Martha is book review editor of *The Lesbian and Gay News-Telegraph*, and under her own name coordinates CLEAR (Community Liaison for Education and Research) providing Lesbian and Gay speakers for the L/G community and the non-L/G community. Her favorite activity is having conversations and coffee, and she would like to learn to levitate.

Fred Flotho lives in San Bernardino, CA. Although he likes to think of himself as retired, he does have to spend time managing and maintaining his rental properties, as they are his livelihood. His main interests are in outdoor activities; he also spends considerable time with the Gay and Lesbian Community Center and the local political action committee. His painful experiences as a gay person whose parents had to move to another state because they could not face having a gay son, plus the fact that one of his sons is also gay, have made him realize how important it is to become visible and to work to overcome ignorance and prejudice in society.

Judith Galas says, "My 42 years have taught me one important lesson — life is full of surprises. As a teenager, I assumed I'd become a teacher, marry my high-school boyfriend, have at least four kids and live happily ever after in a Chicago suburb. I got fooled. After a 14-year marriage, one daughter, moves to Philadelphia, Minnesota and a Montana sheep ranch, I finally grew up to be a Lesbian and a writer. I've been a reporter in Montana, New York, London, and Kansas. Today I share my days with my life companion in Lawrence, Kansas. As to being lesbian — well, all I can say is I'm sure glad I didn't die before I found out."

Judy Helfand is a white, middle-class Jewish lesbian and free-lance editor who loves being a mother. She has always had a lot of support so she's able to get alone-time and breaks from parenting responsibility. She and her lover have been together for nine years; her lover has always wanted to be a good co-parent (with the clear understanding that she doesn't feel the same bond with them that Judy does) and has worked hard to build a positive and rewarding relationship with Luke and Clio. With her, Judy really feels she doesn't have to be 100% responsible for meeting their needs.

Sharon Joyce is a 43-year-old woman living on a farm with her life-partner, 12 cats, and 2 dogs. Organic gardening is their main hobby, and a lot of Joyce's energy in the past five years has gone into the planting of fruit trees, berry bushes, and lots of vegetables. Last year she also planted 300 pine trees and hopes to open a small Christmas tree farm in another five or six years. She says, "It seems odd to me now that I could spend twenty years denying my sexuality, but I am thankful for my sons and am glad it turned out so that they can share this aspect of my life with me."

Susan Llork, an Indianan, grew up in a working-class Catholic family. A high-school graduate, she was married at 21, gave birth to Erich at 25, and came out as a Lesbian at 30. She has worked in clerical and administrative positions in manufacturing for her whole working life. Softball has been a lifelong activity. Sue has been a player, a coach at all levels from pre-teen through college, and a certified high school and college athletic official in softball and basketball; it was at a softball game that she met her lover Donna. Her goals are to become more politically active in Lesbian/gay issues, to retire within fifteen years, and to write Lesbian fiction. Erich thinks it's "neat" that some of his story is appearing in this book.

Loralee MacPike is a Professor of English at California State University, San Bernardino, where she teaches women's literature and children's literature. For four years she has been Review Editor for *Lesbian News,* the largest all-Lesbian newspaper in the country. Currently she is the Pacific Southwest regional coordinator for the National Women's Studies Association and a member of the NWSA Coordinating Council. With her partner, photographer Mary McArthur, she lives in Altadena, CA.

Jacqueline Matthews' multiracial family si a distinct minority in the Florida community where she and her lover live with their three daughters. Jacque has never written for publication before.

Terry Love is the pen name of a California woman. This is her first published work.

Betty Mansfield is a freelance writer whose current work includes public relations for a local hospital, collaboration on an educational filmscript on homophobia, and a monthly column for the gay press.

Shelly Rafferty is a working-class white woman of genuine Yankee heritage writing for something other than her health. She works with parenting teenagers and their beautiful babies and hopes to add to the entourage of infants with one of her own soon. She lives in upstate New York.

Gwynn Sawyer Ostrom is a viticulturist living in Fresno, CA with her horticulturist husband John. Currently she is a research associate in the Viticulture Lab at California State University Fresno and author of several articles on grape culture. In her spare time, she climbs mountains. She is the daughter of Loralee MacPike and Mary McArthur.

Heather Wishik writes: I am a lesbian, a feminist (unmodified), a writer and attorney living in Vermont. Three of my poems appeared under the pseudonym "Esther Hawk" in *New Lesbian Writing,* the 1984 Grey Fox Press anthology edited by Margaret Cruikshank. One of these poems is being republished in *Open Lines,* the St. Martin's Press anthology of gay and lesbian poetry of the last 50 years edited by Joan Larkin and Carl Lewis. My legal articles, which often include poems, have been published in the *Berkeley Women's Law Journal, Family Law Quarterly, New Mexico Law Review,* and *Vermont Bar Journal.* An article about child custody I co-authored with four other people is forthcoming in the *Journal of Child and Adolescent Psychiatry.* I am now writing a novel.

A few of the publications of
THE NAIAD PRESS, INC.
P.O. Box 10543 ● Tallahassee, Florida 32302
Phone (904) 539-5965
Mail orders welcome. Please include 15% postage.

THE BEVERLY MALIBU by Katherine V. Forrest. 288 pp. A
Kate Delafield Mystery. 3rd in a series. ISBN 0-941483-47-9 $16.95

THERE'S SOMETHING I'VE BEEN MEANING TO TELL
YOU Ed. by Loralee MacPike. 288 pp. Gay men and lesbians
coming out to their children.   ISBN 0-941483-44-4   9.95
                          ISBN 0-941483-54-1 16.95

LIFTING BELLY by Gertrude Stein. Ed. by Rebecca Mark. 104
pp. Erotic poetry.   ISBN 0-941483-51-7   8.95
                          ISBN 0-941483-53-3 14.95

ROSE PENSKI by Roz Perry. 192 pp. Adult lovers in a long-term
relationship.   ISBN 0-941483-37-1   8.95

AFTER THE FIRE by Jane Rule. 256 pp. Warm, human novel
by this incomparable author.   ISBN 0-941483-45-2   8.95

SUE SLATE, PRIVATE EYE by Lee Lynch. 176 pp. The gay
folk of Peacock Alley are *all* cats.   ISBN 0-941483-52-5   8.95

CHRIS by Randy Salem. 224 pp. Golden oldie. Handsome Chris
and her adventures.   ISBN 0-941483-42-8   8.95

THREE WOMEN by March Hastings. 232 pp. Golden oldie. A
triangle among wealthy sophisticates.   ISBN 0-941483-43-6   8.95

RICE AND BEANS by Valeria Taylor. 232 pp. Love and
romance on poverty row.   ISBN 0-941483-41-X   8.95

PLEASURES by Robbi Sommers. 204 pp. Unprecedented
eroticism.   ISBN 0-941483-49-5   8.95

EDGEWISE by Camarin Grae. 372 pp. Spellbinding
adventure.   ISBN 0-941483-19-3   9.95

FATAL REUNION by Claire McNab. 216 pp. 2nd Det. Inspec.
Carol Ashton mystery.   ISBN 0-941483-40-1   8.95

KEEP TO ME STRANGER by Sarah Aldridge. 372 pp. Romance
set in a department store dynasty.   ISBN 0-941483-38-X   9.95

HEARTSCAPE by Sue Gambill. 204 pp. American lesbian in
Portugal.   ISBN 0-941483-33-9   8.95

IN THE BLOOD by Lauren Wright Douglas. 252 pp. Lesbian
science fiction adventure fantasy   ISBN 0-941483-22-3   8.95

THE BEE'S KISS by Shirley Verel. 216 pp. Delicate, delicious
romance.   ISBN 0-941483-36-3   8.95

RAGING MOTHER MOUNTAIN by Pat Emmerson. 264 pp.
Furosa Firechild's adventures in Wonderland. ISBN 0-941483-35-5   8.95

IN EVERY PORT by Karin Kallmaker. 228 pp. Jessica's sexy, adventuresome travels. ISBN 0-941483-37-7   8.95

OF LOVE AND GLORY by Evelyn Kennedy. 192 pp. Exciting WWII romance. ISBN 0-941483-32-0   8.95

CLICKING STONES by Nancy Tyler Glenn. 288 pp. Love transcending time. ISBN 0-941483-31-2   8.95

SURVIVING SISTERS by Gail Pass. 252 pp. Powerful love story. ISBN 0-941483-16-9   8.95

SOUTH OF THE LINE by Catherine Ennis. 216 pp. Civil War adventure. ISBN 0-941483-29-0   8.95

WOMAN PLUS WOMAN by Dolores Klaich. 300 pp. Supurb Lesbian overview. ISBN 0-941483-28-2   9.95

SLOW DANCING AT MISS POLLY'S by Sheila Ortiz Taylor. 96 pp. Lesbian Poetry ISBN 0-941483-30-4   7.95

DOUBLE DAUGHTER by Vicki P. McConnell. 216 pp. A Nyla Wade Mystery, third in the series. ISBN 0-941483-26-6   8.95

HEAVY GILT by Delores Klaich. 192 pp. Lesbian detective/ disappearing homophobes/upper class gay society.
ISBN 0-941483-25-8   8.95

THE FINER GRAIN by Denise Ohio. 216 pp. Brilliant young college lesbian novel. ISBN 0-941483-11-8   8.95

THE AMAZON TRAIL by Lee Lynch. 216 pp. Life, travel & lore of famous lesbian author. ISBN 0-941483-27-4   8.95

HIGH CONTRAST by Jessie Lattimore. 264 pp. Women of the Crystal Palace. ISBN 0-941483-17-7   8.95

OCTOBER OBSESSION by Meredith More. Josie's rich, secret Lesbian life. ISBN 0-941483-18-5   8.95

LESBIAN CROSSROADS by Ruth Baetz. 276 pp. Contemporary Lesbian lives. ISBN 0-941483-21-5   9.95

BEFORE STONEWALL: THE MAKING OF A GAY AND LESBIAN COMMUNITY by Andrea Weiss & Greta Schiller. 96 pp., 25 illus. ISBN 0-941483-20-7   7.95

WE WALK THE BACK OF THE TIGER by Patricia A. Murphy. 192 pp. Romantic Lesbian novel/beginning women's movement.
ISBN 0-941483-13-4   8.95

SUNDAY'S CHILD by Joyce Bright. 216 pp. Lesbian athletics, at last the novel about sports. ISBN 0-941483-12-6   8.95

OSTEN'S BAY by Zenobia N. Vole. 204 pp. Sizzling adventure romance set on Bonaire. ISBN 0-941483-15-0   8.95

LESSONS IN MURDER by Claire McNab. 216 pp. 1st Det. Inspec. Carol Ashton mystery — erotic tension! ISBN 0-941483-14-2   8.95

YELLOWTHROAT by Penny Hayes. 240 pp. Margarita, bandit, kidnaps Julia.   ISBN 0-941483-10-X   8.95

SAPPHISTRY: THE BOOK OF LESBIAN SEXUALITY by Pat Califia. 3d edition, revised. 208 pp.   ISBN 0-941483-24-X   8.95

CHERISHED LOVE by Evelyn Kennedy. 192 pp. Erotic Lesbian love story.   ISBN 0-941483-08-8   8.95

LAST SEPTEMBER by Helen R. Hull. 208 pp. Six stories & a glorious novella.   ISBN 0-941483-09-6   8.95

THE SECRET IN THE BIRD by Camarin Grae. 312 pp. Striking, psychological suspense novel.   ISBN 0-941483-05-3   8.95

TO THE LIGHTNING by Catherine Ennis. 208 pp. Romantic Lesbian 'Robinson Crusoe' adventure. ISBN 0-941483-06-1   8.95

THE OTHER SIDE OF VENUS by Shirley Verel. 224 pp. Luminous, romantic love story.   ISBN 0-941483-07-X   8.95

DREAMS AND SWORDS by Katherine V. Forrest. 192 pp. Romantic, erotic, imaginative stories. ISBN 0-941483-03-7   8.95

MEMORY BOARD by Jane Rule. 336 pp. Memorable novel about an aging Lesbian couple.   ISBN 0-941483-02-9   8.95

THE ALWAYS ANONYMOUS BEAST by Lauren Wright Douglas. 224 pp. A Caitlin Reese mystery. First in a series.
                                                         ISBN 0-941483-04-5   8.95

SEARCHING FOR SPRING by Patricia A. Murphy. 224 pp. Novel about the recovery of love.   ISBN 0-941483-00-2   8.95

DUSTY'S QUEEN OF HEARTS DINER by Lee Lynch. 240 pp. Romantic blue-collar novel.   ISBN 0-941483-01-0   8.95

PARENTS MATTER by Ann Muller. 240 pp. Parents' relationships with Lesbian daughters and gay sons.
                                                         ISBN 0-930044-91-6   9.95

THE PEARLS by Shelley Smith. 176 pp. Passion and fun in the Caribbean sun.   ISBN 0-930044-93-2   7.95

MAGDALENA by Sarah Aldridge. 352 pp. Epic Lesbian novel set on three continents.   ISBN 0-930044-99-1   8.95

THE BLACK AND WHITE OF IT by Ann Allen Shockley. 144 pp. Short stories.   ISBN 0-930044-96-7   7.95

SAY JESUS AND COME TO ME by Ann Allen Shockley. 288 pp. Contemporary romance.   ISBN 0-930044-98-3   8.95

LOVING HER by Ann Allen Shockley. 192 pp. Romantic love story.   ISBN 0-930044-97-5   7.95

MURDER AT THE NIGHTWOOD BAR by Katherine V. Forrest. 240 pp. A Kate Delafield mystery. Second in a series.
                                                         ISBN 0-930044-92-4   8.95

TO THE CLEVELAND STATION by Carol Anne Douglas.
192 pp. Interracial Lesbian love story.   ISBN 0-930044-27-4   6.95

THE NESTING PLACE by Sarah Aldridge. 224 pp. A
three-woman triangle—love conquers all!   ISBN 0-930044-26-6   7.95

THIS IS NOT FOR YOU by Jane Rule. 284 pp. A letter to a
beloved is also an intricate novel.   ISBN 0-930044-25-8   8.95

FAULTLINE by Sheila Ortiz Taylor. 140 pp. Warm, funny,
literate story of a startling family.   ISBN 0-930044-24-X   6.95

THE LESBIAN IN LITERATURE by Barbara Grier. 3d ed.
Foreword by Maida Tilchen. 240 pp. Comprehensive bibliography.
Literary ratings; rare photos.   ISBN 0-930044-23-1   7.95

ANNA'S COUNTRY by Elizabeth Lang. 208 pp. A woman
finds her Lesbian identity.   ISBN 0-930044-19-3   6.95

PRISM by Valerie Taylor. 158 pp. A love affair between two
women in their sixties.   ISBN 0-930044-18-5   6.95

BLACK LESBIANS: AN ANNOTATED BIBLIOGRAPHY
compiled by J. R. Roberts. Foreword by Barbara Smith. 112 pp.
Award-winning bibliography.   ISBN 0-930044-21-5   5.95

THE MARQUISE AND THE NOVICE by Victoria Ramstetter.
108 pp. A Lesbian Gothic novel.   ISBN 0-930044-16-9   6.95

OUTLANDER by Jane Rule. 207 pp. Short stories and essays
by one of our finest writers.   ISBN 0-930044-17-7   8.95

ALL TRUE LOVERS by Sarah Aldridge. 292 pp. Romantic
novel set in the 1930s and 1940s.   ISBN 0-930044-10-X   7.95

A WOMAN APPEARED TO ME by Renee Vivien. 65 pp. A
classic; translated by Jeannette H. Foster.   ISBN 0-930044-06-1   5.00

CYTHEREA'S BREATH by Sarah Aldridge. 240 pp. Romantic
novel about women's entrance into medicine.
    ISBN 0-930044-02-9   6.95

TOTTIE by Sarah Aldridge. 181 pp. Lesbian romance in the
turmoil of the sixties.   ISBN 0-930044-01-0   6.95

THE LATECOMER by Sarah Aldridge. 107 pp. A delicate love
story.   ISBN 0-930044-00-2   6.95

ODD GIRL OUT by Ann Bannon.   ISBN 0-930044-83-5   5.95

I AM A WOMAN by Ann Bannon.   ISBN 0-930044-84-3   5.95

WOMEN IN THE SHADOWS by Ann Bannon.
    ISBN 0-930044-85-1   5.95

JOURNEY TO A WOMAN by Ann Bannon.
    ISBN 0-930044-86-X   5.95

BEEBO BRINKER by Ann Bannon.   ISBN 0-930044-87-8   5.95
    Legendary novels written in the fifties and sixties,
    set in the gay mecca of Greenwich Village.

VOLUTE BOOKS

JOURNEY TO FULFILLMENT	Early classics by Valerie	3.95
A WORLD WITHOUT MEN	Taylor: The Erika Frohmann	3.95
RETURN TO LESBOS	series.	3.95

These are just a few of the many Naiad Press titles — we are the oldest and largest lesbian/feminist publishing company in the world. Please request a complete catalog. We offer personal service; we encourage and welcome direct mail orders from individuals who have limited access to bookstores carrying our publications.